Grassroots, Greystones, and Glass Towers

Grassroots, Greystones, and Glass Towers

MONTREAL URBAN ISSUES
AND ARCHITECTURE

Véhicule Press

MONTRÉAL

DOSSIER QUÉBEC SERIES

The publisher gratefully acknowledges the support of The Canada Council and the assistance of Moe Levin.
Special thanks to *The Gazette* for the use of its photographs; and to Susan Bronson, Isabel Corral, Maureen Anderson, and Ricardo L. Castro for their help in the preparation of this book.
Versions of three articles, "Significant Buildings of the 1980s," "The Façade Fad," and "Architectural Heritage: More Than Preserving Old Buildings" have been previously published.
Images utilized in cover: "1001 de la Gauchetière" courtesy of Dimakopoulos & Associés and Lemay & Associés; "New Sherbrooke building" courtesy of Moshe Safdie Associate, Desnoyer Mercure Architectes and Lemay & Associés.

Dossier Québec Series editor: Simon Dardick
Cover design: Pol Turgeon
Editorial assistance: Sarah Brierley
Design and imaging by ECW Production Services
Printing by Les Editions Marquis Ltée.
Published by Véhicule Press, P.O.B. 125, Place du Parc Station, Montreal, Quebec H2W 2M9

Copyright © the authors 1989. *All rights reserved.*
Dépôt légal, Bibliothèque nationale du Québec and the National Library of Canada 4th trimester 1989.

CANADIAN CATALOGUING IN PUBLICATION DATA

Main entry under title:
Grassroots, greystones & glass towers : Montreal urban issues and architecture
ISBN 1-55065-001-7
1. City planning — Quebec (Province) — Montréal. 2. Architecture, Modern — 20th century — Quebec (Province) — Montréal.
I. Demchinsky, Bryan
HT169.C32M65 1989   711'.4'09714281   C89-090325-5

Canadian distribution
University of Toronto Press, 5201 Dufferin Streeet, Downsview, Ontario M3H 5T8

U.S. distribution
University of Toronto Press, 340 Nagel Drive, Buffalo, N.Y. 14225-4731

Printed in Canada.

TABLE OF CONTENTS

PREFACE 7

INTRODUCTORY ESSAY

DANE LANKEN
Montreal: At the New Crossroads 11

URBAN DEVELOPMENT

NORBERT SCHOENAUER
A Skyline for All Seasons 19

LEWIS HARRIS
The MCM at City Hall: Long on Promises,
Short on Action 29

ISABEL CORRAL
The Promise of a Master Plan 40

URBAN SPACES

PETER JACOBS
The Magic Mountain: An Urban Landscape for the
Next Millennium 53

RON WILLIAMS
Recycling the Expo Islands and Lachine Canal . . . 61

DAVID BROWN
The Indoor City: From Organic Beginning to
Guided Growth 70

DEREK DRUMMOND
   Streets Can Be a City's Living Room 83
ALINE GUBBAY
   The Fine Art of Enhancing Public Places 93

ARCHITECTURE

RICARDO L. CASTRO
   Significant Buildings of the 1980s 109
DEREK DRUMMOND
   The Decade of the Designer Tower 119
MARK LONDON
   Postmodernism Comes to Montreal 130

HERITAGE

JOSHUA WOLFE
   Architectural Heritage: More Than Preserving
   Old Buildings 145
SUSAN BRONSON
   The Three Rs: Restoration, Renovation
   and Recycling 154
JOSHUA WOLFE
   The Façade Fad: Saving Face Isn't Always Enough . . 168
PIETER SIJPKES
   The Four Lives of Pointe St. Charles 176

HOUSING

IAN MACBURNIE
   Downtown Housing: Filling in the Gaps 191
ADRIAN SHEPPARD
   Housing That Belongs on Montreal Streets 197

NOTES ON CONTRIBUTORS 211
INDEX 212

Preface

In the summer of 1983, I first met Mark London, who had sold *The Gazette* on the idea of publishing a weekly column on architecture and urban issues.

A relative newcomer to Montreal with no background in architecture, I was assigned to edit the column in collaboration with Mark, an architect who was at the time executive director of Heritage Montreal.

Editing the column has been an invaluable learning experience and has added to my enjoyment of the city. Working with Mark has led me on occasion to refer to him as the David Suzuki of architecture, but behind the quip is a useful observation. Architecture and urban development, like science, are somewhat esoteric subjects, given to arcane language and complex ideas. They are also tremendously important areas of knowledge with immediate and pervasive applications to daily life. To step outside the door each day is to be confronted with the blessings and annoyances of the built environment, especially in cities where most Canadians now live. Mark recognized the value of popularizing the information that shapes this environment and made it his mission to do so.

The same motivation lies behind the creation of this book. Indeed, many of the writers here are those who appear in *The Gazette* column. There are two reasons. The writers are, for the most part, practitioners and teachers in the field about which they are writing. Critical writing on architecture for general audiences in Canada is at an early stage; few people make a living at it, so it is both necessary and useful to turn to those who are most closely connected to the area of discussion. The writers' ideas also represent a consensus. As experienced observers of Montreal, they have discerned patterns of development both positive and negative, and there is considerable agreement about ways that the city's evolution can be guided.

In a book that features 18 articles by 16 authors, there are naturally limitations. The voices are disparate, the tone perhaps uneven. Nor is it possible to give an entirely comprehensive picture of the state of urbanism in Montreal. An attempt has been made to cover much ground, from heritage to the planning process and politics, but Montreal is too large and its urban processes too intricate to be contained in a single volume.

The need to make sense of the urban environment is one reason for undertaking *Grassroots, Greystones and Glass Towers*. Another reason is equally important. Reporting on the 1989 opening of the Canadian Centre for Architecture in the journal *Architecture*, American urbanist John Pastier called Montreal "arguably the continent's finest city," and described it as "an extraordinary and underappreciated city." Pastier was speaking to a wider North American audience, and his words represent one man's opinion, but they have much significance for Montrealers. We need reminders of what makes Montreal a great city, and we must guard against forces that would endanger its liveability. In 1975, these concerns led three journalists at *The Gazette*, Donna Gabeline, Dane Lanken and Gordon Pape, to publish *Montreal at The Crossroads*, which warned against the effects of uncontrolled development. Today, as Dane Lanken explains in this book's introductory article, we are at a new crossroads but facing many of the same challenges.

Bryan Demchinsky

GRASSROOTS, GREYSTONES, AND GLASS TOWERS

Montreal: At the New Crossroads

DANE LANKEN

Many Montrealers felt their city was at a crossroads in the early 1970s. Things were changing rapidly, and the kind of city people hoped for, a city of parks and nice neighbourhoods, of historic buildings and a dynamic downtown, was being lost to parking lots and dull concrete towers.

Worse, the citizenry had no say in which path the city would follow. The mayor, Jean Drapeau, dreamed only of mega-projects. City council was his rubber stamp, and with no controls or master plan, development was haphazard and often destructive. It was not the road to rational growth that was gaining the upper hand, but the expressway to urban ruin.

Finally, the era ended, victim of recession and Referendum jitters and the rise of urban reformists. Now, at the end of the 1980s, those same reformists are in power. And Montrealers live in a city where — Heaven spare us — development is still haphazard and almost no home or historic building is safe.

The 1960s were good times in the City of Montreal. There was prosperity, an expanding population, social peace and optimism. There were bold new buildings like Place Ville Marie, a spiffy new subway system, and in 1967, a fair that brought the world brilliantly, beautifully to Montreal's door. There was pride in the city, and confidence for the future. When Jean Drapeau declared that Montreal would be "the London, the Paris, the great cosmopolis" of the New World, it seemed reasonable and right.

But things went downhill instead. There were bitter strikes and political turmoil, and a 1970 health report found that a fifth of Montrealers lived in poverty. Suddenly it seemed (as author and architect Jean-Claude Marsan observed) that Expo 67 was "neither a beginning nor an ending, but only a spectacle for the moment."

Development still boomed, though. But the quality builders and urban innovators of an earlier era gave way increasingly to hucksters attracted by Drapeau's anything-goes attitude on building and demolition. By the early 1970s, the city was known internationally as a builders' banana republic. Numbered European companies and local hustlers alike routinely assembled downtown blocks, flattened the elegant, century-old greystones on them and sometimes put up second-rate high-rises in their stead.

Governments and institutions were just as rapacious. The province demolished 3,000 homes for the east-west Ville Marie expressway, the federal government 18 entire blocks for the inane Radio-Canada building. McGill University bulldozed a dozen fine homes around its ever-duller and more crammed campus. Even churches and convents were razed, many for highway construction.

Indeed, little of this demolition was of the Baron Haussmann type; he flattened much of Paris a century ago, but put back the broad boulevards for which the city is famous. Here, it was usually for something less attractive: high-rise towers imposed on 19th-century streetscapes, half of folksy Chinatown replaced by a big office building, and on so many of the downtown streets, Bishop, Mountain, Stanley, Dorchester, de Maisonneuve, rows and rows of handsome, serviceable, human-scale, characteristically "Montreal" greystone houses were lost, more often than not replaced by parking lots. It was a case of a city trading away its heritage; for the mayor in hopes of more tax dollars to finance Olympic profligacy; for many developers, in quest of quicker bucks.

Today, of course, many of the greystones that remain have become hot properties, gentrified housing or fashionable shops. I like to believe that the hustler, so intent on demolishing a row of greystones on Bishop below St. Catherine 15 years ago that he got a court order evicting his tenants, now looks across the street from his still-barren lots at the glittering success of a similar still-standing row, and realizes he blew it.

Perhaps the biggest disappointment in the early 1970s, certainly the one that made people feel most powerless, was the Van Horne mansion, the fine greystone home of the great railway builder William Van Horne

Greystones on Dorchester (René Lévesque) Boulevard
near Mountain Street came down during the 1970s.
Photo by Aussie Whiting, courtesy of The Gazette.

October 20, 1988. The Queen's
Hotel awaits the wrecker's ball.
Photo by Len Sidaway, The Gazette.

that stood for 104 years on the corner of Stanley and Sherbrooke Streets. There was widespread support to preserve the house, from the public and from various advisory boards. But public opinion meant nothing. The mayor didn't care and the house was lost. Yet some good came of it. Drapeau's callousness enraged many Montrealers, and grass-roots citizens' groups and new political parties gained ground. Indeed, the downtown ridings that had seen so much demolition never returned a Drapeau party councillor again. And the mayor himself, his I-know-best autocracy finally fading, won his last election in 1982.

New moods among Montrealers, to preserve, to restore, to improve the city, carried the Montreal Citizens' Movement (MCM) to power in the next election four years later. It promised consultation, respect for neighbourhoods and historic buildings, and planned and controlled development.

But somehow, those ideals lost something in the translation to real power.

For one thing, the demolitions continue. The Queen's Hotel (formerly on lower Peel Street), was a lovely and historic building, in poor but salvageable condition. The MCM stood by and let a developer go back on his promise to restore it, and instead, let him knock most of it down in 1989. Now there's yet another bare spot in Montreal's still parking-lot pocked downtown.

The Regent Theatre on Park Avenue, opened in 1916, was the most historic and best preserved golden-era movie palace left in the city. The MCM showed no alarm when the theatre fell into the hands of the developer who had earlier gutted the equally lovely Monkland Theatre, and uttered no protest when the Regent's exquisite paintings and plasterwork were turned to dust.

Then there was Overdale, where a major project was imposed on a quiet downtown street. The MCM threw out everything it had ever stood for — preservation of neighbourhoods and human-scale buildings, consultation and respect of residents' wishes — and backed the developer. The final scenes in the drama, police evicting people from their homes as the wreckers stood by, was worthy of the Drapeau era.

Any of these episodes would have been the perfect occasion for a grand statement of beliefs by the MCM. But it acquiesced to anything, and lost a lot of respect.

There have been other things, too: high-rises in the Square Mile (the pretentiously named Sir Robert Peel being the latest example), a South

Shore commuter train (when the city is already clogged with cars), still no final master plan for city development, and ever more office towers built cheek-by-jowl, creating that "dead zone" look of President Kennedy Avenue and adjacent de Maisonneuve Boulevard. (These same streets open onto the "new" McGill College Avenue, a grand and windswept boulevard that goes nowhere, lined with shiny glass, and in the case of Place Montréal Trust, monumental office buildings, the whole thing strangely alien to Montreal.) It's "a nice Toronto street," says one wag.

So what went wrong with the MCM? Are they too green? Too gullible? Too unused to the real-life rigors of government to stand up for what they believe? Sadly, the city seems a tougher place now, bad drugs, violence in the Métro, surlier drivers and maybe stubborner developers, too. And the MCMers, dewy-eyed, weaned on a single despot like Jean Drapeau, perhaps now find themselves surrounded and out-classed.

Or maybe we were expecting too much, that one change of government would turn a banana republic into a responsibly-run city.

The MCM did set up an extensive citizen consultation system after taking office. But the advice it gets seldom seems to affect what decisions are made.

At this new crossroads in the history of the City of Montreal, glass towers still mean more to the powers-that-be than greystones or grassroots.

URBAN DEVELOPMENT

The city is a constantly evolving entity of immense complexity. Change occurs incrementally in small stages as streets and neighbourhoods wax and wane, and in giant steps as developers and municipal authorities impose large-scale projects that alter the character of familiar places seemingly over night.

How to control the forces of change is matter of continual debate among planners, architects, urban critics and politicians. In Montreal, it has focussed on issues such as the way the downtown and outlying districts develop and on the methods by which change will be directed.

Articles in this section examine the recent urban development of Montreal: a critique of the high-rise downtown, an analysis of the Montreal Citizens' Movement administration's effectiveness in controlling development and a discussion of the uses and limits of a master plan for the city.

A Skyline for All Seasons

NORBERT SCHOENAUER

Like other major cities of North America, Montreal has undergone profound physical changes during the second half of this century. This transformation is most manifest in the inner city, where glossy new high-rise office towers crowd each other for breathing space. The gleaming towers impose a new scale upon the urban environment, and if overdevelopment of these tectonic giants is not checked, the quality of life within the inner city will be adversely affected.

Since its beginning, Montreal's skyline was dominated by the mountain hovering over the city and shielding it from the cold northern winds. Green in summer, grey-white in winter and aglow with many hues in the fall, Mount Royal provided the backdrop for the downtown in the past as it still does today.

But there is a difference. In the past the mountain was clearly dominant over the man-made urban environment nestled at its feet, while today, large-scale high-rise buildings are vying for supremacy. Whether the towers will succeed depends on the foresight of our municipal government and the will of its citizens.

Just as church spires gave identity to the early 19th-century city, so high-rise buildings make distinctive the skyline of the contemporary city. Office towers, in particular, act as visual landmarks of the 20th-century city, and are viewed as symbols of progress and prosperity. Since architecture reflects the values of the society that built it, it is telling that the skyline of Montreal is no longer ruled by church spires but by office towers of banks, insurance companies and large corporations.

The concept of high-rise structures is not indigenous to Montreal.

Originating in Chicago and New York City, high-rise buildings had, at the outset, a modest height in comparison with today's towers. In the 1880s when buildings in New York reached the height of 10 or 12 storeys, the term "skyscraper" was coined, a designation that is now normally reserved for much higher structures. For many years prior to the post-Second World War building boom in Montreal's inner city, the 26-storey Sun Life building was considered the largest office building in the British Commonwealth.

Underlying the evolution of high-rise buildings are two primary forces: maximizing the use of urban land through vertical expansion, and establishing a prestigious presence with a building that preferably soars above everyone else's. Naturally, technological advances made in the building industry were enabling forces that encouraged this evolution. Greater sophistication in structural design and building construction, new types of light-weight curtain-wall cladding and mechanical improvements, such as high-speed elevators as well as pressurization and air-conditioning of buildings, were important technological achievements that made it possible to build ever higher buildings.

In Montreal, there are three distinct generations of high-rise buildings that can be distinguished in the post-Second World War period, each of them identified with a decade and separated from each other by a few years of relative inactivity in the building investment trade. The developments of the 1960s essentially pre-dated Expo 67, those of the 1970s the Olympics of 1976, and the most recent wave of construction, still to peak, celebrates the emergence of a new optimism following the political ferment of the late 1970s and the short, unsettling period of recession and inflation in the early 1980s.

In architectural terms, the 1960s and 1970s were marked by the tenets of Modern architecture and the International Style, while in the 1980s the Modernist and Postmodernist styles have competed for attention.

With its 45-storey cruciform office tower on an elevated plaza oriented toward a recently widened Dorchester Boulevard, Place Ville Marie (1962–66) was planned in the 1950s to be the key structure in a string of new skyscrapers that would form a new city centre. Other projects along Dorchester, since renamed René Lévesque Boulevard, included the 34-storey CIL building (1962) near University Street and the 45-storey Canadian Imperial Bank of Commerce building (1963) at the corner of Peel Street. New skyscrapers also appeared below the Dorchester Boulevard escarpment, such as the 47-storey Place Victoria

Montreal 1989. Office towers are the visual
landmarks of the 20th-century city.
Courtesy of The Gazette.

Place La Laurentienne on René Lévesque Boulevard.
New types of curtain-wall cladding have led to taller buildings.
Photo by A.D. Corsillo.

Set amid the greystones of the Milton-Park
district, La Cité is an example of a large-scale
mixed-use project on the periphery of downtown.
Photo by Shane Kelley, The Gazette.

(1966) and Place du Canada (1967) with a 28-storey office building and the 38-storey Château Champlain Hotel. A unique departure from a high-rise tower concept was 13-storey Place Bonaventure (1967), a multi-use building complex housing a retail shopping centre, exhibition hall, merchandise mart, office complex, and a 400-room hotel surrounding a roof garden.

Before construction started in the late 1950s, the seven-acre Place Ville Marie building site was an unsightly ravine-like cleft with a railway tunnel entrance and a marshalling yard of Canadian National Railways. The air rights for development of this site so near to St. Catherine Street were secured by the promoter, William Zeckendorf, and the complex was built by Webb & Knapp (Canada) Limited. At the time, Zeckendorf, its promoter, hailed the complex as "l'Etoile de Montréal" and, indeed, the plaza with its tall curtain-walled cruciform tower and shopping concourse at its base became a popular landmark of the city.

In the wake of an unprecedented suburban expansion that started in the 1950s, it was widely contended that suburban shopping centres constituted a real threat to the conventional downtown shopping street. But, with the erection of the Place Ville Marie complex these fears were allayed, since its climate-controlled shopping promenade was successful from the very beginning. Its proximity to thousands of office workers and great numbers of commuters using the neighbouring railway station guaranteed success. In fact, this project emerged as a trend-setter and established the initial skeleton of an underground network of walkways flanked by shopping arcades that is still expanding.

Trademarks of most of these high-rise structures included a plaza, curtain-wall construction technology for the office building, some commercial establishments at the base, and a self-conscious insularity that is most manifest in their hostility towards the street. At sidewalk level, most of these buildings do not help much to animate street life, and when they do, it is only to entice passersby to enter their lobby or shopping concourse. An additional annoyance to pedestrians using the streets adjacent to high-rise developments is the adverse micro-climatic effects attributable to them. Not only do they cast their long dark shadows like tentacles upon the surrounding streets and neighbourhood, but they also deflect air currents, resulting in the familiar turbulent wind gusts that make their outdoor plazas and adjacent streets unpleasant, and very cold and disagreeable during the winter months.

The continued fascination with high-rise development is surprising if one considers the additional construction and maintenance costs it entails. Clearly, with increased height the construction costs of building foundations and support structures are disproportionally greater due to lateral wind forces, as well as precautionary measures that must be taken against earth tremors. Fire protection above the reach of fire ladders (about nine storeys) necessitates the use of sprinkler systems that again translate into higher building costs. With increased height the elevator service is also more costly, not only because high-speed elevators are required, but since efficiency demands that they be grouped in banks serving about 10 floors each, resulting in wasted floor areas. Finally, energy efficiency diminishes in tall buildings. With increased height there is a decrease of temperature, an increase of wind velocity and wind chill factor, and an increase of the chimney effect derived from the pressure differential created within tall buildings; all these factors contribute to additional heat loss.

Also disconcerting is the poor economic track record of most of the high-rise building developments that shaped the skyline of Montreal in the 1960s and 1970s. Many of these enterprises experienced financial difficulties in their initial stages and were saved from financial collapse by takeovers.

The most adverse effect of high-rise office building developments upon city life is the loss of vitality in the downtown core when workers empty the buildings after business hours. Office building and commercial land use is much more lucrative in the real estate investment game, so housing in the downtown falls prey to their expansion demands. Yet, residential land use is one of the most important components of a city core that hopes to retain urban vitality throughout the day. The 24-hour use of residential buildings adds life to the street when shops are closed and office buildings deserted; moreover, residents of downtown dwelling units create a sense of safety in the streets due to their presence and self-policing activities. While a few years ago it was still economically possible to build apartment buildings such as the Cantlie House (1964) on the south side of Sherbrooke Street, municipal zoning regulations have made this virtually impossible, except for a few luxury condominium projects.

In New York City developers are rewarded by the municipal government if they incorporate residential land use into office buildings, while in Montreal they are penalized. It is not surprising that housing in the central core is gradually disappearing.

The Canadian Imperial Bank of Commerce
building is a product of the 1960s building boom.
Photo by Tedd Church, The Gazette.

The repercussions of this imbalance of land use will haunt future Montrealers if counter measures are not implemented by city hall.

The second generation of high-rise buildings in the inner city continued the trend of mega-projects, but the height of these towers did not exceed those of their predecessors. While the first generation of tall buildings was endorsed because it was viewed as a symbol of progress, the social cost of displacing low-rent existing housing with high-rent new apartments by the 1970s led to much criticism of downtown development. Another factor that contributed to the popular movement resisting new high-rises was based on nostalgia emanating from the rapid disappearance of a familiar urban environment whose human scale now was gradually being replaced by dehumanizing megastructures.

In the later 1970s and earlier 1980s, a third generation of high-rises shifted development north of St. Catherine Street, along de Maisonneuve Boulevard and McGill College Avenue in closer proximity to the Métro line. Initially, building heights stayed well below those established in the 1950s, hovering around 20 storeys, but recently there has been a tendency to increased building height. This is exemplified by the IBM-Marathon building, which will become the highest tower in Montreal when it is completed in 1991.

Early examples of the third generation of office towers in the inner city are represented by the 20-storey Banque Nationale de Paris, the 24-storey Place Mercantile, and the 22-storey Industrial Life Tower, all flanking the newly widened McGill College Avenue. Essentially, these buildings are pure office towers with only restaurants and newsstands and no shopping concourses at their base. Some more recent office towers are much higher and include shopping malls at their base, as is seen in the case of the Maison des Coopérants with its cavernous shopping centre called Place de la Cathédrale and Place Montréal Trust with its multi-storied atrium-lit shopping arcade.

A significant departure in these two developments is their connection to each other by underground walkways that run parallel with St. Catherine Street. Stretching from The Bay to Les Cours Mont-Royal, this new underground climate-controlled, air-conditioned and neon-lit shopping spine competes with St. Catherine Street, luring people away from the traditional public shopping corridor during store hours and depriving street-level shop owners of exposure to essential pedestrian traffic.

Should this underground shopping spine become very successful, it is conceivable the character of St. Catherine Street will change, perhaps unfavourably.

An exemplary development of the 1980s in terms of urban scale is Maison Alcan, on Sherbrooke Street between Stanley and Drummond Streets. From an urban design perspective, this complex demonstrates the viability of a moderate profile — rather than high-rise — office building that is neither in conflict with the scale of old buildings nor with the functional demands expected by corporate clients. There are several other features here worthy of closer examination. First, Alcan's world headquarters pays homage to Montreal's past by retaining several existing buildings and making them part of the new building complex. Three greystone heritage buildings, formerly residences, were converted into executive offices and a former 10-storey hotel was recycled to serve as a main entrance portal on Sherbrooke Street with office accommodation above. These existing buildings have been given a genuine new lease on life, instead of the popular recent practice of preserving façades as mere stage sets to appease nostalgia, as was done in Place Mercantile a few blocks to the east. Behind the old buildings and linked to them by a soaring atrium is the new eight-storey office wing, the Davis building. With its triple-glazed rainscreen envelope, this building represents the state of the art in curtain-wall design and construction. In spite of the various architectural styles in close juxtaposition, the designers of Maison Alcan succeeded in creating a stylistic harmony between old and new, a feat that was possible because the new buildings were neither overbearing nor subordinate in size or scale to the old.

Although residential land use was unfortunately shunned in all major developments in the downtown area, some large-scale projects at the periphery of the inner city were built as true mixed-use developments. Two such projects from the 1960s were the Alexis Nihon Plaza with the first multi-level shopping concourse around a skylit atrium in Montreal, and Westmount Square, perhaps the city's most pristine example of Modern architecture. Another example of mixed used development, but this time from the 1970s, is La Cité. This complex consists of an office tower, a hotel tower, and three high-rise apartment buildings with a total of 1,352 residential units. A two-level retail mall, partially underground, interconnects the apartment buildings.

The newest phase in high-rise development follows the recent

American trend, described by Ada Louise Huxtable, one of America's most acclaimed architectural critics, as a stylistic "preoccupation with surface" accompanied by "sheer, stubborn disregard for the people and the cities the structures serve." If this trend (discussed in the articles in the following section) continues to be endorsed by our city authorities, Montreal's enviable position of being one of the most lively, beautiful, and safe North American cities will not endure.

The MCM at City Hall:
Long on Promises, Short on Action

LEWIS HARRIS

The Montreal Citizens' Movement will establish clear rules of the game, known by everyone, so that the development of Montreal can continue on a harmonious basis.

— *MCM election promise.*

When the Montreal Citizens' Movement (MCM) and new mayor Jean Doré took power in Montreal in 1986, hopes soared that the city would be delivered from what many citizens saw as two major complaints against the regime the MCM was replacing — uncontrolled development based on decisions made in private.

An open city hall, coupled with intelligent urban planning, were among a handful of key commitments the MCM offered voters as the party sped towards its first-ever municipal election victory since its founding in 1974.

A few weeks before the election, the MCM published what it called a "priority action plan for a first Montreal Citizens' Movement administration." Among the many promises in the plan was one to "establish clear rules of the development game," in part by creating urban plans for all districts of the city.

With so much emphasis on planning, many MCM backers envisaged lively public meetings where citizens would tell a caring city administration what was best for their neighbourhoods. And sophisticated information would be available for citizens, courtesy of the city's planning department.

How would a new project affect available sunlight in the area? Would the project create wind tunnels? How much traffic would a project attract? There would even be aesthetic considerations; how would a new building look in relationship to other buildings around it?

Never more, many Montrealers believed, would huge office and residential towers be foisted on an unsuspecting public, with ordinary citizens left to cope with whatever problems these projects might cause.

Now, with the MCM concluding its first term in office in 1990, many are wondering how much there will be left to save by the time the city gets around to approving an urban development plan. Since taking office, the MCM's performance in planning has been long on public relations and short on action.

The city has tabled proposals for a downtown master plan and has promised a wide-ranging public consultation beginning in January 1990. The final version of the plan is to be approved by city council in June, a few months — conveniently — before the MCM seeks re-election in November. The city also has organized several public consultations on proposals for eight urban plans covering all districts outside downtown. But the MCM says those plans will not be given final approval by Montreal city council until 1992.

The various urban plans, once they are approved, will together form the one, long-awaited master plan promised by the MCM. But critics are quick to point out that any master plan is perfectly useless if it takes effect after a construction boom is over. Montreal has been experiencing such a boom, without benefit of a master plan, since the city pulled out of the recession of the early 1980s. In 1988, after its preliminary downtown plan was unveiled, city council gave quick approval to a handful of multi-million dollar office and residential projects that will change radically the city's skyline. Many of them will be underway way or finished when final approval is given to a downtown master plan.

In fact, 1988 proved to be a watershed year in the life of the city and the MCM. In October of that year, the city said yes to two office towers that will be on the same scale as Place Ville Marie, now the city's most dominant office complex.

PVM's tallest tower rises nearly 188 metres above ground and rivals the summit of Mount Royal for the highest elevation on the city's downtown skyline. Among planners, Mount Royal is referred to as "God's mountain," while the downtown's skyscrapers are "man's mountain."

Planners generally agree that man should not try to outbuild the Creator.

Construction is well underway on one 45-storey tower, a joint project by Marathon Realty Co. Ltd. and IBM Canada Ltd. on René Lévesque Boulevard between Stanley and La Gauchetière Streets. It is expected to cost $250 million by the time it opens in 1991.

The second project, a 51-storey building, is being built by Prodevco Immobilière, BCE Development Corp. and Teleglobe Canada in an area between Place Bonaventure and Place du Canada. The $250-million project is expected to be completed by the fall of 1991.

In April 1988, council also gave quick approval to a $200-million, 31-storey office tower and shopping complex, known as the Centre Eaton, at St. Catherine Street and McGill College Avenue. The project, scheduled to open in the fall of 1990, was approved despite protests from the Save Montreal heritage group, which charged that factors such as wind tunnelling and access to sunlight had not been adequately studied. Retail outlets in the York-Hannover project will open in 1990. The office tower, to be put up by a yet-to-be identified second developer, is expected to be finished a year later.

Another 24-storey condominium and shopping complex was approved for Guy and St. Catherine Streets in the block that includes the York Cinema. And City Arboretum Corp. is putting up a 19-storey condominium project at Guy Street and de Maisonneuve Boulevard at a cost of around $40 million. The project is scheduled for completion in early 1991.

Most of what passed for public consultation on these projects occurred when they were debated at city council meetings. But the MCM administration, elected with 55 of the city's 58 council seats in 1986, has been able to use its huge majority to steamroller what little opposition there was at city hall.

Denis Marchand, an architect and lecturer in urban planning at the Université de Montréal, believes the city has been too timid in dealing with developers. The "neophyte" MCM administration may have had good intentions, but it quickly became "so frightened of chasing away investment capital that it approved major projects far too quickly," he said.

Marchand also said the city should have undertaken in-depth independent impact studies for each of the major projects, rather than relying on the city's planning department, which is not known for rigorous impact evaluation. (For example, a city impact study on sunlight and shadows created by the Centre Eaton was done on June 21, the longest day of the year.) The studies might have forced developers to wait a year or two at the most but would not have forced anyone to cancel a project entirely, Marchand said. The delay also would have permitted more input from citizens.

Dinu Bumbaru, executive director of the preservation group Heritage Montreal, offered a similar view. The MCM administration, Bumbaru said, has "shown us that it wants to do something, but we're still waiting for a downtown master plan." Without such a plan, he said, it is damaging to race ahead with major projects. Bumbaru said the MCM administration should have slapped a freeze on new downtown projects until a master plan was completed.

Bumbaru also believes the city's planning department cannot meet the challenges of modern-day urban planning, mostly because the MCM has failed to live up to an election promise to beef up the department with more staff and resources. City planners are expected to produce impact studies on wind, sunlight traffic and parking whenever a developer seeks the city's approval for a new project. But because of understaffing, the reports often read like hieroglyphics, Bumbaru said.

The Université de Montréal's Marchand is particularly worried about how the Centre Eaton project could change St. Catherine Street. Until now, buildings in the area of the proposed development have been no taller than eight or nine storeys. That made the street a haven for outdoor shoppers and one of the few remaining places where independent retailers could set up shop. A 31-storey structure would tower over St. Catherine Street and deprive it of its liveliness by draining people away to indoor shops that would be part of the project, Marchand said.

Other critics say the MCM administration should have demanded socially useful amenities such as low-cost housing, greenspace and daycare as a tradeoff for permission to put up a major project.

Not everyone is entirely negative in assessing the MCM's performance so far in urban planning. MCM city councillor Arnold Bennett, usually one of his own party's severest critics, says it would have been unreasonable to expect the city to freeze all development for the minimum three years needed to produce a coherent, downtown development plan. Instead, the MCM passed an interim bylaw shortly after it came to power, placing a blanket height restriction on all new downtown buildings. Exceptions were granted on a case-by-case basis. The bylaw was used to size down the IBM-Marathon and Prodevco towers to 45 storeys from an initially projected 60 storeys each, so that they would not interfere with a view of Mount Royal. And the tower atop the Centre Eaton — initially approved by the Civic Party administration that preceded the MCM — will be built 27.4 metres back from St. Catherine and McGill College to minimize the project's impact on St. Catherine Street.

The MCM's seeming diffidence toward the big developers was echoed in its weak-in-the-knee public consultation policy. The creation of neighbourhood District Advisory Committees (DACs) to advise city council on issues to come before it has been of little use so far on urban planning issues. The DACs only came into existence in the summer of 1989, well after major projects were approved by council. But the DACs, whose recommendations are non-binding, will be used to study the proposed master plans for districts outside the downtown area.

The MCM administration also has shown itself to be accident-prone at the types of things the party was supposed to be able to do well: protecting the city's tenants, its heritage buildings and its greenspace.

Signs that something was amiss within the MCM were there early, for anyone willing to interpret them. One indication of the party's change in orientation occurred just as the MCM was taking over at city hall. The scene was the Bonaventure Hotel, November 18, 1986. Jean Doré was to be sworn in the next day as mayor, Montreal's first new mayor since the election of Jean Drapeau 26 years earlier. It was Doré's first major speech since winning the mayoralty. He was guest speaker at a Chambre de Commerce de Montréal luncheon, with most of the city's business elite anxious to hear what the mayor-elect had to say.

Doré did not disappoint them. He left no doubt that he wanted the city to maintain its comfortable relationship with Montreal's business community. The mayor told the businessmen that the newly elected MCM administration would try to take advantage of a growing sense of entrepreneurship among Montrealers. Later, he told reporters that the MCM's platform was "perfectly in tune with the mood and dynamism of the Montreal business community."

Doré sounded a little like a past president of the Chambre as he rattled off a series of his administration's concerns: getting the new Canadian Space agency located in Montreal, promoting bio-technology industries in the city and helping the garment industry. (The space agency eventually went to St. Hubert).

Mayor Jean Doré (right), John Gardiner and the
MCM were elected to city hall on the promise
of more carefully planned development.
Photo by John Mahoney, The Gazette.

Boarded-up greystones on Overdale Avenue
a year after the tenants were evicted.
Photo by Tedd Church, The Gazette.

The mayor and other members of the administration were anxious to prove themselves no enemy to business. John Gardiner, one of six people named to Doré's executive committee, also wanted to shed whatever lingering doubts there were about his ability to perform in office.

Before the MCM assumed power, Gardiner was known as a blunt and outspoken populist; someone party members could count on to defend them against bullying landlords or greedy developers. He was one of the MCM's most popular leaders. Gardiner had a talent for organizing successful housing cooperatives. So Gardiner's appointment to the city's executive committee, with responsibility for housing, planning and development, seemed natural enough. The powerful, seven-member executive committee functions much like a federal or provincial cabinet and meets in private.

Gardiner's personality changed little at city hall. But the same traits that won him friends before the election seemed to get him into trouble afterward. MCM supporters who remembered Gardiner fondly for his outspoken ways soon began referring to him as him as stubborn, uncompromising and unwilling to admit error.

Gardiner's problems began in the summer of 1987, in what seemed like a moment of triumph for the young MCM administration. Gardiner stepped into a burgeoning dispute between a group of tenants and two developers who wanted to build twin, 39-storey towers as part of a $100-million condominium development. The project, which became known as Overdale, would be built on the south side of René Lévesque Boulevard between Mackay and Lucien L'Allier Streets.

Developers Robert Landau and Douglas Cohen, in the best tradition of press-release hyperbole, billed their development as "world class." "A star is born at the corner of Mackay and Dorchester," they proclaimed.

The only problem was a group of 70 tenants living on Overdale Avenue, a pleasant street running parallel to René Lévesque. The street can barely be seen from René Lévesque because it is slightly downhill from the busy thoroughfare. Because of their secluded location, Overdale and a few nearby streets formed one of the city's few remaining downtown residential neighbourhoods.

Sixty or so apartments would have to be demolished along Overdale to make way for the project, forcing the tenants to move. Not all of the tenants were willing to go. The developers owned virtually all the land

and buildings in the area. They did not require a zoning change from council to go ahead with their project. They appeared to have the city and tenants living in the area at their mercy.

In June 1987, Gardiner held meetings with Landau and Cohen and the tenants. He emerged with what he thought was a first-class deal: For the first time in North America, Gardiner said, developers of a large project had voluntarily agreed to build $1 million worth of new housing to replace the apartments they would be knocking down. Better still, the developers would give the housing to the city for free. Tenants affected by the project could live in brand new apartments. Rents would be higher than the tenants had been paying, but still far below market values. Gardiner described the agreement as "not Shangri-La, but it's almost perfect."

It didn't take long for the nearly perfect deal to come unravelled. By August, a vocal, well-organized tenants association adept at dealing with the media announced they did not want to move — ever. The tenants, about half of the original 70 living along Overdale, ignored several eviction notices, some of them from the city's fire department, whose inspectors said many of the apartments contained too many fire hazards for continued occupation.

Support for the tenants picked up. They got help from several quarters, including housing groups, other tenants associations as well as from high-profile members of the city's architectural heritage community such as architect Michael Fish and Phyllis Lambert, founder of the Canadian Centre for Architecture. A handful of MCM city councillors, including Bennett, Marcel Sevigny, Marvin Rotrand, Sam Boskey and Pierre Goyer marched with the demonstrators. (In part because of the Overdale experience, Boskey, Goyer, Rotrand have since left the MCM). They all believed the MCM administration was betraying a sacred duty to protect tenants. After all, tenants groups were among the founding members of the MCM. What could be more fundamental to the MCM than protecting tenants' rights?

Media from across the city were on hand when the MUC riot squad showed up in March and June of 1988 to evict the handful of tenants who still had not left their homes. Few MCM supporters missed the brutal irony conveyed in the television images: an MCM administration, in power two years, had called in the riot squad — helmets, nightsticks and all — to haul away the MCM's traditional constituents and send them to jail. Some protesters were treated roughly as they were pulled or shoved into police paddywagons, although police generally acted with restraint.

"Overdale was a disaster," Bennett maintains. "The tenants were deported. A neighbourhood was gutted. There's no project and the neighbourhood will be an eyesore for years. It's a continuing black eye for the administration."

On Oct. 4 1988, workers tore down a three-storey apartment building in the Overdale area to complete a weeks-long demolition to make way for the luxury condominium project. A year later, Lisa Jensen of the Overdale Tenants' Association held a news conference to mark the anniversary of the demolition of the buildings. Nothing has taken their place.

Landau and Cohen emerged from the fracas just as embittered. The developers met the city's demands for replacement housing and were the first ever to do so, they have often pointed out, only to be vilified for their efforts.

Their replacement housing was derisively nicknamed "Underdale" since it is located downhill from the original apartments. Half the tenants who could have moved there decided to go elsewhere.

Delays caused by court cases and a city administration that failed to give the developers all the required backing meant that competitors got a head start in the condominium market, the developers complained. With the condo market gone soft, the developers have no plans to build their project before they are legally obligated to or before the market changes. A city bylaw gives Landau and Cohen until September 1990 to start construction and another five years after that to finish work. The Overdale condominium site, now occasionally used as a parking lot, could stay much as is until the middle of the next decade.

Critics say the city, and Gardiner in particular, made several errors in their handling of the project. There should have been more consultation with the tenants before the city gave its approval for the project. The word "secret," often used to describe how projects were approved during the Drapeau era, now is used to describe how Gardiner reached agreement with the developers and tenants. And more of an attempt should have been made to make the tenants and the buildings they lived in part of the new project.

As the controversy continued, members of the MCM's social-democratic grass-roots argued that by shunting the tenants into replacement housing, the city was turning the condominium project into a rich-only bastion. A mixed-income project would have been preferable.

Gardiner, however, still touts the Overdale project as one of the MCM administration's accomplishments while in office. In a poll of party members, however, the Overdale project and the handling of the tenants involved in it emerged as the MCM's biggest flop since coming to power.

Overdale wasn't the only embarrassing run-in between the city and its new-found friends in the development industry. In the summer of 1988, the city agreed to allow demolition of the former Queen's Hotel, a handsome red sandstone structure built in 1892 that had been boarded up since 1977.

Although the building at the corner of St. Antoine and Peel Streets didn't evoke the splendour of grand city hotels such as the Windsor or the Ritz-Carlton, in its heyday it had been an important railway hotel (across the street from the now-demolished Bonaventure Station) catering to the city's middle class. Its redstone façade was one of the last of its kind in Montreal, making the Queen's a heritage building that cried out for some sort of protection.

Reports from city engineers said that the building was so structurally unsound that it posed an immediate danger to anyone working or walking near it. Council then gave the go-ahead to developer Solly Karkoukly to knock down most of the building.

Ironically, the opposition Civic Party, which earned a pro-development reputation during its 26-year term in office, led the fight to save the Queen's. The Civic Party took the city to court to try to block demolition. The courts said no. The wrecker's ball began its work on October 27, 1988. The demolition that would take months to complete as Karkoukly and the city went through the rubble, trying to recuperate and classify whatever looked valuable. Today, a minor remnant of the Queen's remains standing. Nothing has been built on the rest of the site.

Yet another embarrassing incident occurred when the city barged ahead with plans to lay down artificial turf in Jeanne Mance Park on what had been a dirt and grass football field. Residents living on Esplanade Avenue facing the park complained that they had not been consulted and did not approve of the change to one of the city's few remaining truly green, greenspaces.

Once again the city found itself in court. And once again, the city won. But it's a winning streak made up of Pyrrhic victories as the MCM comes to terms with the wording, spirit — if not heart and soul — of its commitment to improve Montreal through intelligent urban planning.

And it's a winning streak that is costing the MCM dearly in more tangible ways: so far, five city councillors elected in 1986 under the MCM banner have now quit the party and are sitting on opposition benches at city hall. The departures of MCM veterans Sam Boskey, Pierre Bastien, Pierre Goyer, Pierre-Yves Melançon and Marvin Rotrand were the result of disagreements on several issues, not just planning.

But those five, and their supporters, could be actively involved in setting up a new party to fight the MCM in the 1990 election. No doubt, any new party they form will make urban planning a key plank in its election platform.

The Promise of a Master Plan

ISABEL CORRAL

Montrealers have for decades lamented the dearth of urban planning in the city. Indeed, during the Drapeau years, a comprehensive approach to planning did not exist. The city developed along more or less organic paths, its growth mediated by economic, political and social forces, with city hall providing only minor legislative intervention. In some respects, the city did not appear to be the worse off for it. Perhaps even more so than it is today, Montreal during the 1960s and early 1970s was a popular city, considered to be a good place to live.

Increasingly, however, Montrealers have become concerned with the effects unplanned development is having on their city, and there have been many calls for a master plan to guide the city's future growth. The underlying belief is that with planned development, Montreal will become a better place to live.

Without guidelines, development in the past was carried out largely in reaction to specific problems or opportunities, regardless of public or professional opinion. In many cases, this approach has had detrimental consequences. One has only to recall the demolition of Goose Village (also known as Victoriatown) in the early 1960s. Found at the foot of Cité du Havre, this community of about 300 families was considered to be an eyesore for visitors to Expo 67. Goose Village's destruction came about despite studies commissioned by the Drapeau administration that found the community was closely knit with fewer health problems and a higher percentage of homeowners than similar working class neighbourhoods elsewhere in the city. While renovation subsidy programs were being prepared for the city (1965–67), the poor physical condition of the housing was given as the main argument for demolition.

Little Burgundy, just southwest of the downtown core, was dealt a similar blow in the 1960s when most of the homes in the area were demolished to make way for public housing. After a few blocks were rebuilt, the remaining land lay vacant for years until the city launched Opération 10,000 logements (later expanded to Opération 20,000 logements), offering subsidies as an incentive to build new housing. During the intervening years, most services left the area.

The construction of the Ville Marie expressway in the 1970s came at the expense of neighbourhoods in the east end of downtown and in lower Westmount. Most of the land in the east end remained vacant for years until the highway was extended as a boulevard in 1988.

With the prosperity of 1950s and early 1960s, it seemed to matter less. As architect Ray Affleck noted in the 1975 book *Montreal at the Crossroads*:

> "During the early 1960s, the development of Montreal was masterminded by a skillful mixture of people, controlled and directed by a happy combination of public and private corporations . . . . unfortunately, the same level of good luck and judgment does not exist this time around. In the past, Montreal has always developed in a climate of consensus. But now a polarization is taking place, with the developers on one side and the preservationists on the other. The business community is acting as if it had to destroy all the existing values on, for example, Sherbrooke Street, in order to create new ones. We must get away from this polarization, from childish economic determinism on one side and 100 per cent preservation on the other. The city should be taking the lead here, but we are not doing our political homework. We are not getting political leadership in this area." (*Montreal at the Crossroads*, p. 17)

Affleck's words heralded a change in attitude that was soon made politically manifest in Montreal. Based on a growing awareness of the value of lively neighbourhoods, architectural heritage and abundant green space, a new consensus was formed. Its beginnings were found in the grass-roots opposition to Drapeau and in the heritage conservation movement that arose in the wake of the Van Horne mansion demolition. The guiding principles of groups formed out of the new consensus were that citizens should have more say in the future of their city and that rational decision-making an impact assessment of urban planning be included in the development process. Ultimately, these ideas gained political legitimacy when the Montreal Citizens' Movement (MCM) came to power in 1986. Many people felt the time had come for ideas to give way to action, and a master plan for the downtown was to be a primary vehicle.

The Purpose of a Master Plan

The MCM platform has always maintained the need for a master plan, that is, a statement of desired goals and objectives that would guide land use for the city. Such a document would, if properly conceived and implemented, provide the basis for rational, informed decision-making for long-term development.

A master plan (also known as a comprehensive plan) has two major characteristics. It must cover an entire city, town or region, and it must address the broad and evolving range of issues associated with an area's development, including physical, social and economic concerns dealing with land use, circulation, housing, architectural conservation, public facilities, recreation, safety, etc.

There are five stages in preparing a planning program:

— Basic research is done on the areas affected.
— Long and short-term goals and objectives. Often, these grow out of what is identified as good or bad in the city.
— Further research into the areas affected follows.
— A plan is then prepared.
— In the final stage, it is implemented and evaluated.

While the responsibility for preparing and implementing a master plan lies with the municipal government, it is usually created by professionals after various groups and interests have been consulted. The community often plays an important advisory role in the preparation of plans, and a general statement of community goals and objectives allows a planning agency to express the values of citizens and interest groups.

Plans should attempt to indicate how private and public action can achieve common goals for a 10 to 20-year period. A plan should not be

An east-end neighbourhood was destroyed in the
1970s to make way for the Radio-Canada Building.
Courtesy of the Gazette.

With its monumental buildings,
Sherbrooke is rated as a prestigious street.
Photo by Len Sidaway.

Lively streets like La Gauchetière in Chinatown are
promoted in the preliminary master plan for downtown.
Photo by Richard Arless Jr., The Gazette.

considered a rigid design for the future. Most successful master plans have a high degree of flexibility built in.

Proper implementation is of extreme importance. Without it, many plans become ineffective. It is at this point that political will plays a crucial role. While urban planning professionals must put together a good plan, it is up to politicians to ensure that it is carried out.

Potential and Constraints of Master Plans

Master plans have been popular since the Second World War, having been used extensively in Europe and North America. In Europe, they served to rebuild war-ravaged cities. In North America, they laid the groundwork for the popular suburban developments of the 1940s and 1950s and as the basis for the grandiose urban renewal schemes of the 1960s. After decades of hoping that master plans were the answer to our planning problems, urban planners have finally acknowledged that they are not cure-alls for a city's ills.

Properly implemented, they can keep the worst from happening and save on basic infrastructure costs by ensuring areas are developed in an orderly fashion. They can also guide development.

For example, in the early 1980s when an attempt was made to make Crescent Street into a pedestrian mall, the experiment failed because it was rooted in the belief that pedestrian malls, such as Prince Arthur Street, were universally popular, and not on an analysis of the activity in the area. If city officials and retailers on the street had realized that Crescent's success was due to the fact that people love to cruise the street (where else are there traffic jams at 3 a.m.?), they would probably have left the street open. In itself, a master plan might not have helped them reach this decision, but base studies would have brought out reasons why people are attracted to the street.

The planning profession has acknowledged that a good plan must recognize the particular character of an area, avoiding sterile, mechanical intrusions. Often, unplanned areas that evolve spontaneously have a special appeal and play an important role in anchoring a community. These areas should not be suppressed, but rather supported and integrated into a plan.

In Montreal, the Main is a good example. St. Laurent Boulevard is interesting because of the way it has evolved over the years. Symbolic and geographical dividing line between the French and English cultures, it has always catered to various ethnic groups. During the 1950s and 1960s when banal supermarkets were the rage, the Main kept its specialized grocery shops. While trendy shops come and go, Slovenia, Schwartz's and the Sunshine Garment Company hold their ground. A good development plan would acknowledge the role the Main has played and encourage its continuation.

The MCM's Planning Statement

With the election of the MCM in 1986, many felt that the city was embarking upon a new phase, one where citizens — in direct contrast to the centralized authority of the Drapeau era — would join in the administration's decision-making process.

Following up on one of its campaign promises, the MCM set about preparing a planning statement for the central area — the first phase in creating a comprehensive plan for the entire City of Montreal.

Usually, a city prepares a master plan for its territory as a whole. In Montreal's case, the municipal adminstration chose to prepare a plan for the central area first, and work on the plans for eight other districts in a second phase. This approach makes sense considering how long it is taking the MCM to develop a comprehensive plan for just the downtown and the enormous amount of development that has gone on there during its mandate.

The city's planning statement for the central district, presented in March 1988, states that planning should be people-oriented, that it should reinforce Montreal's particular identity and finally, that it should contribute to economic growth. From these general principles came three main recommendations:

> — The central business district should expand towards the south and east. Such a policy would bring into the downtown orbit the financial district of Old Montreal and the area east of Bleury Street encompassing Place des Arts, St. Denis Street, the Université du Québec à Montréal, etc. At the same time, it was recommended that high-rise buildings be restricted to the area's core, with a gradual decrease in height toward the periphery, thereby maintaining the city's present skyline.

— "Lively" and "prestigious" streets were to be encouraged. Lively streets are those considered special because of their ability to generate activity through their shops, cultural attractions or heritage value. St. Denis, St. Catherine and Crescent Streets are examples. Complementing these streets are major thoroughfares such as Sherbrooke Street and René Lévesque Boulevard, which are lined with monumental buildings.

— Sectors within the central area were to be consolidated, revitalized or developed. Areas to be consolidated were the older ones, already built up to a large degree and therefore not subjected to major changes. Other sectors, such as Faubourg des Récollets, west of McGill Street, were to be revitalized. These areas, having fallen prey to urban decay, are made up of parking lots, abandoned or underused buildings, yet still manage to retain a certain character and established activities. According to the planning document, they should be enhanced to attract new development that complements existing uses. Most of the areas slated for renewal lie in the southern part of the central area.

Besides the main recommendations, discussion was given to five themes perceived as particularly significant to Montreal: urban design, architectural heritage, access to downtown, public spaces and public facilities.

The Next Step

While the municipal government has responded to criticism that not enough long-range, comprehensive planning has been done, it remains to be seen whether its steps are appropriate. Until a master plan is implemented it will be difficult to judge if improvements are being made.
The work done to date has produced a planning statement for the central area, but no mechanisms to implement the proposals. Also unknown is what input the community will be allowed as follow-up to the initial consultation that was conducted after the preliminary plan was made public in the summer of 1988. Will the public be able to respond, not only to the plan, but also to the way it is implemented?

A lag of over two years is foreseen between the presentation of the planning statement and the adoption of the master plan for the central area. Final approval of the plan was originally to have been given in 1989 and has now been rescheduled for June 1990. The plans for the eight districts outside the city centre are to follow in 1992. This is not an inordinate amount of time, considering the many steps that must be taken in producing a plan. More disturbing is what has been happening during this time.

The planning statement did not present interim measures to guide development while the main plan was completed. As a result, Montreal is going through a building boom in which development has not been in keeping with the spirit of the planning statement.

The MCM did pass a bylaw intended to serve as an interim control. Under it, all but the smallest development proposals were to be regulated with plan d'ensembles, a procedure developed during the Drapeau administration. A plan d'ensemble sets aside existing regulations so that each development proposal is considered separately and judged on its suitability, quality, etc. The bylaw gave the MCM administration the power to ensure any development was in keeping with the planning statement's intention.

It appears that the politicians have, for the most part, chosen not to exercise the powers the plan d'ensemble process has given them. A study conducted in 1989 for Heritage Montreal by planning student Nick McDonald looked at 12 major downtown building projects given the green light during a 12-month period under plan d'ensembles. These projects were approved after the planning statement for the central area had been made public, and after indications that the city would use its proposals as guidelines for development while waiting for the master plan to be adopted.

After analyzing the manner in which projects were adopted and whether they respected the interim bylaw, restrictions on height, parking requirements, sun access and pedestrian concerns, the study concluded that no real improvements over the Drapeau era had occurred in the way projects were approved. The study revealed, for example, that several new projects were going to exceed height and density restrictions recommended in the preliminary plan. The floor area ratios (FAR) — the ratio between the total square footage of a building and the area of a property — exceeds 10 in four of the projects. The planning statement suggested maximum FARs of 7 or 8.

There is nothing inherently wrong with plan d'ensembles. It is in their implementation that they break down because there is no framework (legislation and implementation mechanism) to support them. The process is used extensively in North American cities, but within the framework of an existing master plan.

Initially, the MCM gave Montrealers hope about the way the city was developing. That hope is quickly being replaced by the impression that very little has changed in the planning field. While it appears that the professional and technical work on a master plan will be carried out, the political will to make it work is lacking.

Conclusion

A master plan for Montreal should be based on what is successful in our city, on what people like and dislike, on what makes the city more liveable and what takes away from its liveability. After identifying these elements, mechanisms must be found and implemented to enhance the good qualities and eliminate the bad ones.

No plan can predict the future. The city is a complex stage with numerous actors playing roles in complex relationships with cumulative effects. It is unrealistic to think that a comprehensive plan, no matter how good it is, will respond to all situations and solve all problems. But it can help the city enormously by providing a solid base to make development decisions.

So we come back to the question: Can a master plan make Montreal a better city? It can if it is rooted in Montreal's history and culture, if it is flexible enough to respond to an evolving city, and if the political will exists to implement it. The planning statement has provided us with a solid base from which to prepare the plan. If planners and politicians learn from their mistakes in this first attempt and if politicians conscientiously work to ensure the goals of a master plan are met, the future development of Montreal will be enhanced.

URBAN SPACES

Every city has distinctive features that create its unique identity. These include major natural and man-made landmarks, as well as smaller, less evident physical attributes.

In Montreal, the mountain and the river give primary definition to the city, while Place Ville Marie and the silhouette of St. Joseph's Oratory on the mountain's slope are part of the city's human signature. Add to these the smaller parks, buildings, monuments and streetscapes that lend texture to the urban fabric.

How best to foster the use and development of urban spaces both large and small is of immediate concern to Montrealers. The future of Mount Royal and the Expo Islands is now being decided while debate continues about the ongoing development of the Lachine Canal, the indoor city and other public and private places.

The Magic Mountain: An Urban Landscape for the Next Millennium

PETER JACOBS

The St. Lawrence River is the base and Mount Royal the symbolic centre of Montreal. The river and the mountain have always served as landscape references for human settlements, from the Indian village of Hochelaga, visited by Jacques Cartier in 1535, to the vast expanse of our present urban community.

Mount Royal is one of the monteregian hills that punctuate the St. Lawrence River flood plain between the foothills of the Laurentian mountains to the north, and the Appalachian mountains to the south. Despite its relatively small extent and vertical elevation, the three summits of this hill dominate the cityscape. The verdant cover and elevation contrast with much of the fabric of human settlement that surrounds it. This contrast and its perceived importance are such that the hill has always been called, affectionately, a mountain. Successive populations have prayed, built, played, walked, and celebrated holidays and festivals on the mountain in different ways, at different times of the day and night and in all seasons.

Most Montrealers identify the mountain with Mount Royal Park. Yet, the mountain shelters a great deal more, including a unique and extensive combination of the natural and cultural heritage of Montreal.

An Architectural and Landscape Heritage

Many of the early French religious and secular institutions that ring the base of Mount Royal were established during the early 1800s when seminaries and hospitals moved to the foot of the mountain to recapture the space and tranquillity that characterized their original settlements near the St. Lawrence River.

In the mid-1800s public institutions such as McGill University settled against the southern face of the mountain as did members of the newly established "haute bourgeoisie," which included industrialists, lawyers, judges, and successful entrepreneurs. During this period two new rural cemeteries were established in Montreal; the Catholic Notre-Dame-des-Neiges Cemetery, and the Protestant Mount Royal Cemetery. Both continue to nestle in the valleys among the mountain's three summits. Later, in the 1930s, the Université de Montréal was sited on the northern face of the mountain where it has continued to expand ever since. This extensive architectural landscape around the base of the mountain provides an exceptionally rich historical and cultural frame for Mount Royal Park.

Happily, the designation of the architectural landscapes around the foot of the mountain as "heritage sites," protected under law against inappropriate renovation and development, is a healthy and positive sign that both the public and private sectors of Montreal society recognize the value of the unique cultural and natural landscapes of the mountain. We can now begin to focus on the conservation and appropriate use of the mountain precinct, stressing activities that support the established identity that the mountain represents.

The mountain's public park was designed by the most celebrated landscape architect of his time, Frederick Law Olmsted. His presence and ideas add luster to the importance and even magic that the mountain represents in the minds of Montrealers and all those who have visited it. He proposed a program for the mountain park that stressed passive recreation and the progressive discovery of nature and views of the city as it unfolded along the winding paths that led gradually toward the summit of the mountain.

Olmsted's many urban parks are characterized by a design vocabulary that consists of woods, fields, and water. In the vast majority of his work, the original landscape was substantially modified, sometimes even radically, to achieve the desired effect. The design for the park on Mount Royal is an important exception to this practice. In fact, his plan for the mountain landscape provides an excellent example of "sustainable development": using the mountain and its plants and animals only to the extent that their continued health and future is assured.

Mount Royal lookout circa 1915. Mount Royal remains one of the city's biggest tourist attractions.
Notman Photographic Archives.

Mount Royal and its environs provides an all-season playground for Montreal.
Photo by Gordon Beck, The Gazette.

In the 1920s, Mount Royal was a prominent
backdrop for downtown Montreal.
Notman Photographic Archives.

Today, high-rises block views of the
mountain from most parts of downtown.
Len Sidaway, The Gazette.

Sustaining the Mountain Landscape

The conservation, restoration and care of the flora and fauna of the mountain is the most critical component of any program for its use and enjoyment. Yet, there is a long history of neglect, misuse, and even abuse of the forest cover. The mountain park may owe its very existence to one such abusive act. In 1868, a Monsieur Lamothe, one of 11 owners of mountain properties, clear-cut his forest stand during a particularly cold winter. The visual scar on the mountain so outraged the public that the city was pressured to expropriate the land for the purposes of establishing the mountain park. The cost amounted to $1 million, raised between 1869 and 1875, largely through public subscription. By 1920, Marie Victorin, the father of modern biology in Quebec and the founder of the Montreal Botanical Garden, remarked that two-thirds of the forest cover had been lost from the mountain. During the Depression, Frederick Todd, a landscape architect who trained in Olmsted's office, proposed a labour-intensive scheme to dig out and build a pond on the mountain. Excavation revealed that beaver dams had been built on the site many hundreds of years ago, and thus Beaver Lake was established. The black, humid soil recovered from the lake was used to cover the exposed roots of the trees on the mountain; this saved, at least partially, the mountain flora.

Although other periodic attempts to maintain and enhance the forest cover have been initiated in the past 50 years, no structured policy, program or budget has been developed to assure the continuous management of the forest cover. Without such a commitment, the park and other sites on the flanks of the mountain face a perilous future as we approach the next millennium.

Building an Institutional Partnership

Realistically, the mountain is but a terribly small hill amid the extensive, highly urbanized flood plain of the St. Lawrence River. The number of mountain visitors has grown from a few hundred to many thousands, and these people are using the mountain for a wide variety of activities not envisioned when the park was designed. The wear and impact on Mount Royal's ecosystems is considerable. Yet, as the type and extent of use has grown, the commitment to management has declined, threatening to turn the mountain into just another over-used green space.

To avoid this future, the 19th-century mountain park will have to adapt to the realities of the approaching 21st century. We must invent new systems that reflect our aspirations and historical heritage. Part of this challenge must continue to be met within the public sector. As this book was being prepared, the City of Montreal was preparing an overall master plan for the protection and enhancement of Mount Royal. A specific strategy for the restoration and improvement of the park will provide a framework for future management of its forest, fields and wildlife.

The proposed strategy includes a number of initiatives, all of which are intended to reinforce both the mountain's natural and cultural attributes.

First and foremost, Mount Royal provides the only urban vertical relief in the St. Lawrence River plain. The fragile ecology of the mountain, including the older woodland areas and marsh, must be protected. At the same time, a wide variety of active and passive recreational activities inspired by the mountain should be encouraged.

The mountain is also a superb place to learn about nature and the ingenuity of human civilization. Creative programs interpreting this rich heritage must be encouraged for all age groups; for Montrealers as well as for visitors.

The mountain is a unique visual landmark in the city and region of Montreal. Yet we can easily mask this symbol, screening views to and from the mountain, by creating walls of high-rise buildings that would effectively cut the link between the river and the mountain that has sustained the image of Montreal for hundreds of years. The mountain, screened behind a wall of high-rise buildings, will rapidly shrink to insignificance.

The public sector cannot achieve this ambitious program without the active help and participation of the religious, educational, health, corporate, private, and volunteer associations that are actively concerned about the development of the mountain.

A number of encouraging experiments for expanding the management network of the mountain are already in place. The Centre de la Montagne, a non-profit group, has developed exhibitions and other interesting educational programs open to the public for a number of years. Les Amis de la Montagne, another voluntary non-profit organization, has for a number of years articulated objectives for the use of the mountain and will initiate a privately funded campaign to renovate the Smith House. (Built in 1858, it is the only remaining symbol of the time when the mountain was privately owned.) Representatives of the major educational, health, and religious institutions that occupy the mountain now meet regularly with the city to discuss common goals and objectives for the management of the mountain landscape and mutually acceptable ways of achieving them. The cities of Outremont and Westmount have been invited to join this group, which promises to be an unusual and, one hopes, successful experiment in co-operative and participative management.

A focus on the entire mountain, rather than the strict limits of the public park, forms the core of emerging proposals to maintain and improve the whole Mount Royal environment. Through negotiated agreements with adjacent municipalities, institutional partners and a variety of community groups, the original plan for a public park can be expanded. An example is the idea of opening semi-public institutional lands for wider public use. Initiatives such as this warrant support.

With its three summits in three municipalities, access to Mount Royal and the nature of its transportation systems are critical components of its management and design. The mountain is surrounded by a ring of Métro stations that serve as public gateways from all directions. Bus lines from these stations to the various summits of the mountain are easy to imagine, and a shuttle bus providing constant public access to and from the various activity centres is not inconceivable. The main route of automobile access to the mountain is, of course, the Camilien Houde parkway, which bisects the mountain from the east to the west. Originally, this route was a simple foot path; later it was transformed into a streetcar line. This gentle and public system of transportation was developed in the 1930s and replaced in the 1960s by the more aggressive broad and rapid autoroute known euphemistically as the "mountain road." While the road was considered to be at the back door of the mountain park, it is in fact at the very centre of an integrated mountain landscape. For this reason it must be remodelled so that it becomes less a "Caesarean section" and much more a gentle "park avenue," lined with trees and places to pull off the road to view the mountain or the changing vistas of the city below.

For historical reasons, pedestrian access to the mountain has been from the south, where the city started its growth. No equivalent path exists from the north, in part because the public and institutional nature of this side of the mountain developed much later than the southern face, in part because access is very steep. However, views from the north side to Lake St. Louis and to the Laurentian mountains are truly breathtaking. The walk in or between the cemeteries to the mountain park is relatively flat, set within a tranquil, culturally rich environment.

Just as it will take an important commitment by the city to redesign the east-west expressway across the mountain to make vehicle access less intrusive, a cooperative and innovative effort will be required to develop a north-south pedestrian axis across the mountain.

It is conceivable that these pathways will meet at the base of the Mount Royal summit lookout, close to the Smith House. Surely, a creative solution to parking can be found, so that the area adjacent to the house can serve a more appropriate purpose. It is an excellent opportunity to rehabilitate a key location on the mountain. The parking area's central location could serve as an important "living room" for the entire mountain complex. The loss of asphalt is unlikely to be mourned by many.

A wide range of other opportunities can be imagined within the expanded field of the mountain landscape. These include: a pedestrian circuit linking a range of lookouts that would provide a 360-degree panoramic view of Montreal; a peripheral pedestrian circuit at the base of the mountain that would provide routes for joggers or walkers other than those filled with the traffic and noise of the city; a variety of active and passive programs designed to help discover and understand the natural and cultural history of the mountain; and a broad range of recreational and social activities compatible with the mountain's ecology.

While not every city has an Acropolis, everywhere urban regions exist there are landscapes that have symbolic presence; landscapes that are recognized and revered by those who live in their shadow. Mount Royal is such a landscape. Its importance extends beyond its physical boundaries, for it gives definition to the city's identity. Like those before us, we face the challenge of sustaining the mountain's landscape heritage for the future while enjoying its gifts in the present.

Recycling the Expo Islands and Lachine Canal

RON WILLIAMS

Montreal's Expo Islands and the land along the Lachine Canal are examples of the recycling of strategically located urban space after its initial use has become inappropriate. In the case of the Expo Islands, a long military career was followed by conversion to parkland and subsequently by the creation of Expo 67; since that time, a new role has been sought for the site with mixed results, and it now seems to be moving towards a coherent development plan.

In the case of the Lachine Canal, like the Vieux Port an abandoned vestige of Montreal's halcyon days as Canada's maritime gateway, a series of recreation and restoration-based park developments have provided Montrealers with a variety of pleasant and useful environments; the only sour note is that while water is the central element — as with the Vieux Port and the Expo Islands — it serves only as a visual resource and is not used for boating or other activities that would fully exploit its potential.

The Expo Islands — Early Years

The nucleus of the Expo Islands is Ile Ste. Hélène, a natural fortress dominating the Saint Lawrence River directly opposite the Port of Montreal. It is not surprising that this wooded island was fortified as a military outpost for the defence of the city in the early 19th century, when American invasion was still very much a possibility. In the years following the American Civil War of 1861–65, it became apparent that the armies of our southern neighbours were not to be directed northwards, and, following the lead of New York and other progressive cities of the time, the now-available land was set aside in 1874 as a public park for use by the City of Montreal. At that time, Ile Ste. Hélène was easily accessible by boat from the city, still largely concentrated on the riverfront, and the park was heavily used. In fact the island was much easier to get to for picnics and social activities than was the more distant Mount Royal Park, begun in 1877.

Yet the park remained largely "unimproved" with few facilities for visitors until the Depression years, when the federal and provincial governments combined their resources to create an employment creation project that was to realize both the recreational and the historic potential of the site. The project proceeded in parallel with other outstanding park work in the 1930s. Undertaken with unemployment as a spur, public spaces such as the Montreal Botanical Garden and Beaver Lake on Mount Royal were created. For the Ile Ste. Hélène project, Canada's outstanding landscape architect of the time, Frederick Todd, was called upon.

Todd, originally from the United States, lived and practiced in Montreal from 1900 until his death in 1947. He created a vast number of landscape and urban design projects during his career, including Battlefield Park at the Plains of Abraham in Quebec City, the grounds of the Saskatchewan legislature, the plans for the Town of Mount Royal and other large residential areas and parks in every province.

Todd directed the extensive grading and planting, road-building, construction of new buildings and reconstruction of historic buildings that give the island its character today. He relied on the native stone from the island's quarry to establish a "family resemblance" between new and old buildings, thus creating the coherence so much admired on Ile Ste. Hélène (and which has been so hard to achieve elsewhere on the islands and in the port). Todd's designs were not, however, all realized: in his original scheme of 1931, he proposed to reclaim the low-lying islands and shoals near Ile Ste. Hélène to create a series of lagoons and secondary islands, connected by paths and bridges, sheltering both a small boat harbour and a swimming area. This scheme, which prefigured both the plan for Expo 67 and the 1989 "beach-park" project on Ile Notre Dame, indicates the breadth of Todd's vision.

Ile Ste. Hélène and Ile Notre Dame (upper left)
as they appeared about the time of Expo 67.
Courtesy of The Gazette.

The Lachine Canal has become one of the most
widely-used recreation areas in the city.
Photo by Pierre Obendrauf.

Expo 67 and Its Aftermath

The finest hour of the islands was undoubtedly Expo 67, the world exposition hosted by Montreal in honour of Canada's centennial year. Starting in 1963, Ile Ste. Hélène and the surrounding secondary islands, bars and shoals were combined and transformed into the two large islands we know today, including the newborn Ile Notre Dame. Access to the islands was also greatly simplified by the construction of a station on Montreal's fledgling Métro system and the new Pont de la Concorde linking the islands to Mackay Pier.

Expo was an incredible success in so many ways that one cannot imagine Montreal — or Canada — without it. It created a symbol of pan-Canadian pride, became a source of enjoyment for millions, put Montreal on the map internationally, and fostered any number of creative experiments such as Habitat 67 and the geodesic dome of the U.S. pavilion.

But we easily forget its achievement in design terms: the creation of a rich and stimulating urban environment for the pedestrian, integrating an exuberant variety of buildings, modern gadgets such as the "minirail" and traditional elements such as the network of canals into an ensemble through the use of consistent and elegant landscape design, lighting, and site furniture. While Expo was a major impetus to architecture and city planning in Montreal and Quebec, its impact on landscape architecture and industrial design was even more decisive. For many people, this was their first experience with the work of practitioners of either discipline. It was no accident that in 1968, academic programmes in landscape architecture and industrial design were established within the School of Architecture at the Faculté de l'aménagement, Université de Montréal, and both disciplines have since become autonomous schools within the faculty.

This remarkable success had a lot to do with the way Expo was planned — a multi-year collaboration between expert administrators and creative designers in a stimulating atmosphere of teamwork and innovation. In subsequent years, the Expo Islands have not always benefitted from the same level of reflection and action; in fact, the very success of Expo 67 made it extremely difficult to establish a viable future for the islands. Those parts of Expo that were intended to remain have proved very successful, particularly La Ronde amusement park which has been recently refurbished by the city's Parks Department. But the understandable desire to keep alive the spirit of Expo in Terre des Hommes permitted many "temporary" pavilions to deteriorate before our eyes instead of retaining their magic in our imaginations.

In the decades of the 1970s and 1980s, the Expo Islands became (like the Vieux Port) a site for everyone's favourite project, and a number of more and less appropriate installations were built. The Lac des Régates at the southern end of Ile Notre Dame was severely truncated to create the Rowing Basin for the 1976 Olympics, and the creation of the Piste Gilles Villeneuve for the Canadian Grand Prix auto race further altered the site. Both these installations have, however, attracted a loyal following and contribute to Montreal's international reputation. A more environmentally fitting project was the international flower exposition, Floralies 1980, which has since become an attractive floral park. Among the many exhibits created for the Floralies, the Jardin de la Tourbière (a transplanted peat-bog from northern Quebec) has been a favourite. Many other activities and projects have come and gone, or, like the Parc Agro-alimentaire, proposed in the early 1980s, have been planned but never realized.

Current Developments

At present the islands are being restudied by a number of working groups, with a view to creating a new master plan which, it is hoped, will be as exciting and well-integrated as that for Expo 67. The stated goals of the master plan team, led by architect Mark London, are to encourage the development of the full potential of the islands in terms of cultural activities, recreation, tourism, and economic contribution. An important part of the plan will be the integration of the various activities and installations proposed into the natural environment in a harmonious way. The planning team, which includes representatives from several city departments including parks, municipal engineering and buildings, is ably backed by an advisory committee of landscape architects and environmentalists from outside the administration: Peter Jacobs from the Université de Montréal, Michael Hough from Toronto and Don Graham from Ottawa.

The future plan will almost certainly focus on water as a theme; after all, the site is not only surrounded by it, but some 40 per cent of the surface of Ile Notre Dame and a considerable area of Ile Ste. Hélène are occupied by water bodies. This focus is certainly evident in the major project currently under construction on the islands: a beach park at the southern end of the Lac des Régates, designed to accommodate some 6,000 Montrealers in an environment that recalls the Laurentian lakes to the north, both in the character of the landscapes created and in the design of the chalet and other buildings. This project, which is scheduled to open on June 24, 1990, represents the fruition of one of the first campaign promises of Mayor Jean Doré. It features the exploration of a number of new environmental approaches, particularly the use of a "filter lake" in which native plants help to maintain water quality by absorbing and utilizing what would usually be considered impurities in the water.

Overall, the comprehensive approach through which the islands' transformation is being prepared augurs well for their future prospects, and Montrealers can hope that this remarkable site will once again fulfil its potential as a cultural and recreational feature as it did so well during Expo.

The Lachine Canal — Key to Montreal's Growth

The Lachine rapids can be considered as a principal raison d'être for Montreal's founding in 1642: the barrier to navigation they created meant that the Island of Montreal became a natural site for a transhipment centre and settlement. The idea of a canal to bypass the rapids and facilitate transportation to the west was developed very early on by Dollier de Casson, the French engineer who established the first plan for Montreal's streets and squares in 1672.

Montreal's industrial development was dramatically enhanced by the opening and enlargement of the Lachine Canal from 1825 through 1844. Dug through the low, swampy valley that divided the island of Montreal on a roughly east-west line, the canal became the focus of new industry both through access to water transport and through the energy provided by the locks. New residential areas sprouted alongside the factories, housing in often appalling conditions the thousands of workers who arrived from abroad or from rural Quebec throughout the 19th century.

Jean-Claude Marsan, in his book *Montreal in Evolution*, speaks eloquently of the "picture of gloom" which this industrial valley became, in both environmental and social terms. During the 20th century the canal experienced a gradual decline in use; the need for more modern facilities and the development of larger ships led to its replacement by the St. Lawrence Seaway in the 1950s.

Transformation of the Canal: Industry to Recreation

As the canal and adjacent urban areas fell into disuse during the 1960s, several federal government agencies became involved in managing different portions of the canal lands and began to see the potential this remarkable site offered for recreation and historical restoration. In the early 1970s, Public Works and Parks Canada received a mandate to explore this potential and to prepare a master plan for the redevelopment of the canal. Following an exhaustive series of studies that prepared the ground for this plan, a number of proposals were made and many of them were carried out.

Some of the new developments have turned out to be spectacular successes; in particular, the bicycle path, which runs along the canal along most of its length as a sort of modern equivalent of the old "chemin de halage," has proved to be immensely popular. The lack of other types of vehicles and of cross traffic, the experience of a natural environment and the presence of water have made this route the preferred recreational bicycle path for Montrealers. In fact, the bikeway idea came along at just the right moment, as recreation patterns in North America swung away from active, team-oriented sports towards informal, fitness-oriented activities in the late 1960s and 1970s. These new forms of recreation are often "linear" in nature — cycling, jogging, cross-country skiing — and the recreation corridor offered by the Lachine Canal proved ideal for their enjoyment.

A second big success has been the complex of historical restorations at the western end of the canal in Lachine. Meticulously studied and reconstructed by Parks Canada and set in well-landscaped surroundings, historic buildings and other installations evoke the fur traders and pioneers of older days. Not all results have been positive, however. One of the biggest mistakes was the blocking of the eastern end of the canal at its entrance into the Vieux Port. As a result, the one form of linear recreation that is not offered by the canal is the most obvious, that of boating, which is such a popular activity in locations as diverse as the urban canals of London and the Trent-Severn waterway in Ontario.

Further problems have arisen in integrating the continuing and new industrial uses into the developing recreation environment. An interesting example is the failure of the recent (1970s) postal sorting station to make any gesture towards the canal. The building resolutely turns its back on the urban waterway, losing an opportunity to enliven the experience of those travelling along the canal as well as those working within the building.

Present Challenges

Besides the successes noted above, which were the result of governmental initiatives, another new and positive development is now taking place, this time from within the private sector: the old run-down factories and residential buildings in the vicinity of the canal are being gradually recycled for a variety of new urban functions. These include everything from condominiums, such as the Corticelli project, to conversions of old three-storey brick warehouses into office and exhibition spaces. This is urban renewal at its best, one step at a time and requiring a minimum of public funds (primarily guidance and encouragement).

Another exciting development just coming into view is the almost inevitable complete reopening of the eastern end of the canal, as a consequence and corollary of plans to redevelop the Vieux Port. Several schemes have been proposed for this unique site over the years, none of which elicited strong public or private support; but the time now seems ripe for its use as a location for major public buildings. The reopening of the canal will also bring us closer to its use as a resource for recreational boating.

All proposals for the canal, however, must come face-to-face with the difficult water quality issue. There are several feet of various natural deposits and industrial waste products at the bottom of the canal throughout much of its length. Cleaning these out would be extremely costly, time-consuming and perhaps dangerous. In light of the present concern for the environment, there is no assurance that sites to dump this material could be found locally or even abroad. It seems likely that some technique of covering these wastes with impervious materials will be adopted, except in key locations where full removal would be necessary. This would then permit the whole question of water quality to be seriously approached.

The Lachine Canal is already Montreal's classic example of how an abandoned, underused environment can be recycled for positive urban use. If some of the major stumbling blocks noted above can be overcome, and there is every indication that this is possible, the canal, like the Vieux Port and the Expo Islands, can realize its full potential.

The Vieux Port

No discussion of Montreal's water-based recreation areas would be complete without mention of the Vieux Port, the old waterfront stretching from the outlet of the Lachine Canal on the west to the Faubourg Québec on the east. The gigantic area offered by its massive piers, created by landfill over a period of centuries, combined with its proximity to Old Montreal, offer a unique opportunity to create a first-rank urban waterfront with a great variety of activities, oriented both to Montrealers and tourists.

Perhaps the very richness of these potential uses has prevented effective decisions about the future of the port from having been made. Anything and everything has been proposed (and sometimes constructed) for this site, from housing to restoration of the harbour's form in the great days of the 19th century. Now, some 20 years since the area's original use was abandoned and the first design studies for its redevelopment were undertaken, the port's future finally seems to be coming into focus.

A series of public hearings held in late 1985 identified a broad degree of consensus concerning the future role of the site: It should remain public; it should be essentially an open-air recreation area, and it should reflect Montreal's maritime heritage. Throughout the spring and summer of 1989, two design competitions were held to identify the specific proposals that would achieve these goals; well-known international environmental-design firms were invited to compete, along with five similar groups from Montreal. At the time of publication, the Vieux Port Committee was on the point of announcing the winners, and developments should proceed rapidly thereafter. The story of this project will therefore have to be told in a future book on Montreal's urban development.

The Indoor City: From Organic Beginning to Guided Growth

DAVID BROWN

The casual visitor to Montreal could easily miss one of its most famous features. I speak of the "Indoor City," a pedestrian network represented on maps by shaded areas that look like a series of tarantulas flattened on downtown Métro stations or major public buildings with orthogonal tentacles extending in all directions.

This web of corridors presents an interesting example of at least three ideas that have been popular at one time or other in city centre development: the separation of pedestrian and vehicular traffic, the attempt to revitalize city cores with the construction of massive multi-purpose centres that have plenty of retail space, and the recent trend toward private-public partnerships in development.

Dubbed the "Underground City" because the key links with the Métro and between blocks are below grade, Montreal's system is generally taken to include all buildings that may be directly entered from the Métro without going outside. But as this definition includes both below and above grade spaces, some of which have good daylight exposure (the atrium of Complexe Desjardins, for example), the term "Indoor City" seems more appropriate.

The importance of the indoor network has not gone unnoticed. The system has been written up in numerous books and each year architects, planners, developers and city officials from around the world visit to judge its merits for themselves. With the proliferation of "indoor cities" throughout North America, Europe and more recently Japan, it is safe to say that Montreal's has served as an important international model for urban development.

For the most part, the reviews have been good. Visitors are often impressed by the extent of the network, the animation and variety provided by the store-lined corridors, the presence of several large enclosed public places, the cleanliness of much of the system and the overall feeling of security. These qualities are appreciated by residents as well. More than 250,000 people use the system daily, and it is seen by many as an appropriate response for a city with harsh winters.

At the same time a number of concerns have been raised by visitors and residents alike. These involve some of the most fundamental issues in urban design, beginning with the central purpose of cities, which is to provide a place for people with divergent experiences and expectations to meet and exchange information and goods. The history, form, functions, ambience and administration of the indoor environment have an influence on this central role and affect the ways the city is used and perceived. These aspects of the Indoor City are discussed in this essay and several planning guidelines are offered that may be helpful in reviewing new projects to extend the system.

The Privatization of Public Space

Underground Montreal was officially inaugurated in 1962 when the Place Ville Marie tower was completed over an open trench that had been used for many years by a Canadian National suburban commuter railway line. The new centre incorporated shopping below grade level that was directly linked with Central Station. Despite initial difficulty leasing space to skeptical merchants, the practicality and economic viability of this arrangement was soon apparent. Many of the tens of thousands of commuters who used the rail line daily at that time were delighted to have the chance to pass directly from the station platform under a major boulevard to Place Ville Mariee and on towards the main retail core of the city along St. Catherine Street. The fact that these corridors were lined with boutiques was seen as a plus. The shops provided visual variety and animation in contrast to the drab façades of most underground passages leading to and from subway stations in other cities during this period.

The idea of enclosed store-lined passages, however, did not begin with the Montreal development. This concept can be traced back at least to Roman markets and emerged, also, in the form of covered bazaars in early Islamic cities, as arcades in 19th-century Europe and as the ubiquitous suburban shopping centre during the 1950s in North America. Even the idea of providing different levels for pedestrians and vehicles originated 500 years ago with Leonardo da Vinci and was magnificently represented in the plans prepared for the Crystal Way in London in the 1860s, which included different levels for subway trains, store-lined pedestrian routes, offices and residences all covered by a glass arcade. Johann Geist's book, *Arcades*, presents a thoughtful analysis of the emergence of this building type.

The Place Ville Marie development, nonetheless, was important for at least two reasons: it is a magnificent multipurpose centre that stimulated a renaissance of development in downtown Montreal, and it marked an important shift in the type of space that fulfilled the essential city function of providing a locus for exchange. City streets and squares had for centuries offered a place to see and be seen, to strut and compare notes on latest fashions. While these spaces were often adjacent to shops and institutions, and a symbiotic relationship was established between civic and commercial functions, they were undeniably public places. With the construction of Place Ville Marie and the growth of enclosed pedestrian passages that followed, the "city" moved indoors. These new spaces are ostensibly open to the public and to a large measure fulfil "public" functions; yet in the final analysis most of the Indoor City was developed for commercial reasons and is privately owned and operated, resulting in a collage of jurisdictions and what has been called "the privatization of public space."

The growth of the Indoor City over the past 27 years has been phenomenal — due largely to the initiative of individual developers. Extensive passages extend from each of the six Métro stations located in the downtown area. These link directly with 1.7 million square metres of office space, 1,400 boutiques, two department stores, 3,800 hotel rooms, 11,500 parking spaces, three concert halls, two rail stations (Central Station and the Bonaventure commuter station) and numerous housing units. These figures, which are based on official Montreal tabulations and fieldwork by McGill University students, represent approximately 35 per cent of the office space and 30 per cent of the boutiques in the downtown area. The possibility of connecting with the system is now a vital concern for all major projects that contain retail functions. Many extensions to the system have been proposed and are currently being studied by the city.

Impressive as they are, these raw figures do not reveal the full impact of the system. This is because the Indoor City has proved to be more attractive for particular types of stores. For example, a study of commercial establishments within the central area completed in 1980 by planner Ian Cross found that while the percentage of stores without street entrances increased from 2.7 per cent in 1961 to 36.1 per cent, the respective shift for shoe stores from outdoors to indoors is 0 to 48 per cent and for women's clothing 1.8 to 67 per cent.

Consequently, the profile of retail establishments remaining on the street has shifted as well. In recent years there has been a noticeable increase in the number of video game arcades, striptease bars and fast-food outlets along St. Catherine Street. These shifts have led to a great deal of concern about the viability of Montreal's best known commercial street, although for the moment it still supports a good variety of commerce and attracts a high volume of pedestrians. Just north of St. Catherine, however, along de Maisonneuve Boulevard and President Kennedy Avenue, inward-looking corporate buildings ignore the street and create a drab pedestrian environment. As the Indoor City expands, the effects of the mega-domes that were envisaged in the 1960s to cover entire cities may come to fruition — and the attending social, economic and environmental consequences, both revered and feared, will have to be dealt with.

Passing Through, Shopping, or Simply Being There

Since its inception, the Indoor City has served primarily a transportation function. Consequently, it is quite natural that Central Station and the six Métro stations located in the core area provide the basic structure for the system. Each day they collectively pump tens of thousands of people onto the station platforms who are then funnelled through a combination of tunnels, store-lined corridors, atriums and perhaps outdoor sidewalks on their way to their destinations.

While all Métro stations have at least one entrance that is owned and operated by the Montreal Urban Community Transit Corp. (MUCTC), commuters make extensive use of the network of corridors built by private organizations. The latter network includes basically two types of space: corridors, that although privately owned, are designated as entrances to the Métro system and are generally kept open for transit

Network Future –

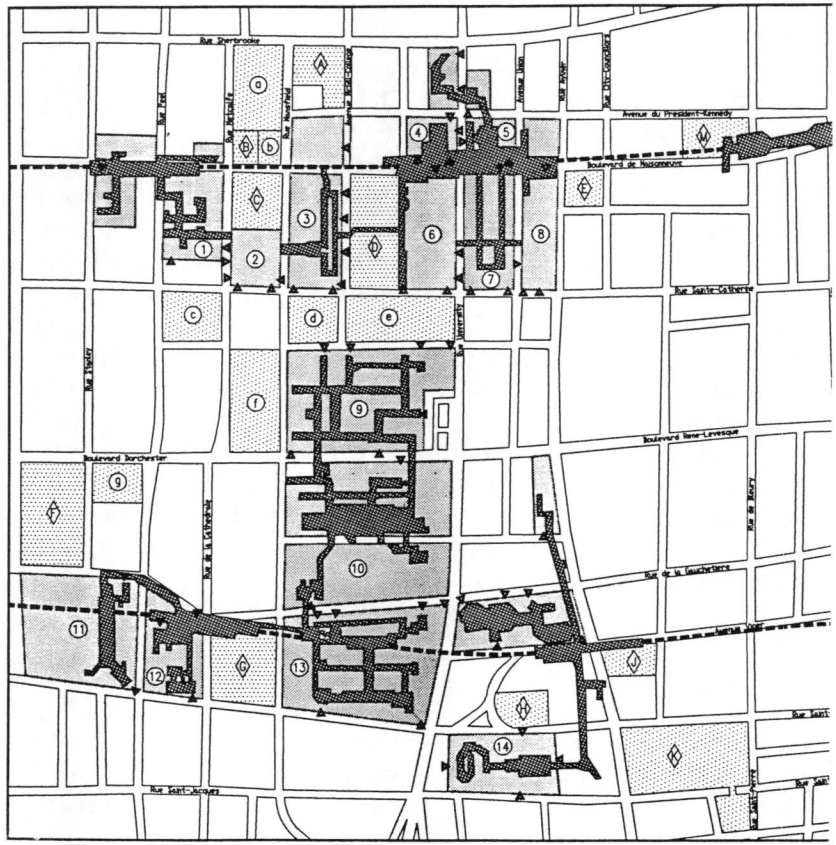

MONTREAL's Indoor

*Map by Kathleen Parewick, courtesy of
McGill School of Urban Planning.*

Snapshot 1989

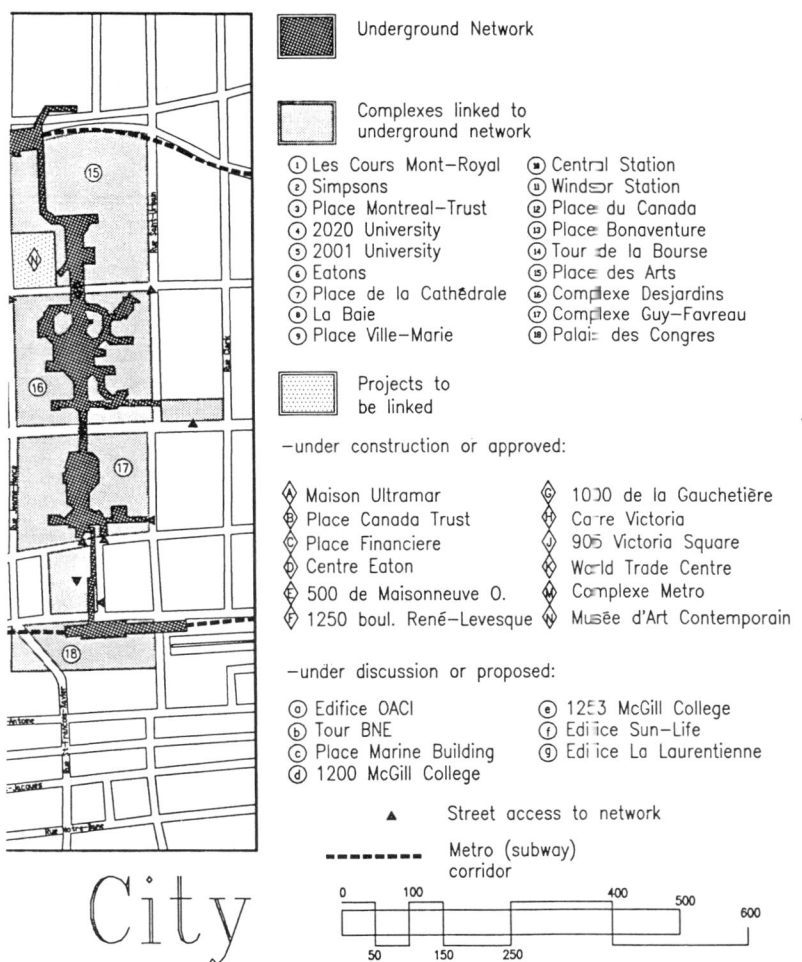

City

users whenever the Métro is in operation, and private stores or centres such as Eaton's or The Bay, which are accessible only during their regular business hours. This distinction has contributed to one of the great pluses of the system. In contrast to many above ground-floor systems that are open only during business hours and require pedestrians to find their way among racks of merchandise, much of the Montreal system is open from 5:30 a.m. to 1 a.m., if not 24 hours, and there is a clear delineation of pedestrian and retail space.

One of the reasons for the growth of the indoor system is the fact that the two Métro lines serving downtown were deliberately located just outside the main commercial and business centres in the city. This has generated a high demand for linkages from de Maisonneuve Boulevard toward St. Catherine Street and from Viger Avenue and La Gauchetière Street toward René Lévesque Boulevard. As the distance between the two lines is about 750 metres and can be easily walked in 15 minutes, it was only natural that the enclosed pedestrian system would link stations on the two lines. This process has created two primary axes: Bonaventure Métro-McGill Métro, which will soon be completed and is almost exclusively privately owned; and a public or para-public route linking Place d'Armes Métro with Place des Arts Métro.

The great volume of pedestrians is, of course, of interest to retailers, and the many commercial centres that are directly linked with the Métro do their best to turn these pedestrians into consumers. General ambience, signs, the selection of stores and the configuration of corridors are all designed with merchandising in mind. Naturally enough, this goal is occasionally in conflict with the transit function of the system. Many centres try to maximize the amount of time that pedestrians spend in their part of the system by down-playing signs that would direct potential clients to other destinations. Place Bonaventure, 2001 University, 2020 de Maisonneuve and the Place Montréal Trust shopping mall are among the more notorious at forcing pedestrians along circuitous routes to gain maximum exposure to their merchants' wares.

On the other hand, shopping has emerged as a major function of the Indoor City in its own right. This is especially evident in the McGill-Peel area where, prior to the closure of Simpson's, three department stores and 550 boutiques were linked. With another 150 boutiques in the planning stage as part of the new Centre Eaton, this facility is effectively a mega-size shopping centre that can surely compete in all aspects, except parking, with any regional mall. Once the Simpson's closure is resolved it may be expected to help retain or even expand the retail prowess of the city centre. In the meantime, it serves as a vivid reminder of the vulnerability of a network that relies on private businesses to provide linkages.

A third function of the Indoor City is its role as a public place where residents and visitors can see and be seen. This function is in part generated by commercial centres that want to be seen as the place to be. There is as well, however, a natural conflict between management's desire to maximize sales and its interest in providing a truly public amenity. Many centres effectively screen clientele by keeping a watchful eye out for "undesirables" and "undesirable activity." Occasionally these definitions may go so far as to embrace all non-shoppers and all non-shopping activity. Observations and interviews indicate that people who would like to spend a little time relaxing in these centres often must adopt a "resting from shopping" attitude when seated. Even then, the guards at many locations are instructed to move people along when they have sat for more than 15 minutes.

The Indoor City in Montreal is fortunate in having two centres that attempt to provide a reasonable approximation of an indoor public square — Complexe Guy Favreau and Complexe Desjardins. Both incorporate a large central space which may be used for a variety of public functions ranging from exhibits to public performances. Complexe Desjardins, in particular, has achieved a certain reputation as a community focus to the extent that groups of seniors are bused in from regional centres such as Trois Rivières to see particular events. In fact, this centre has a steady clientele, especially older men, who use the facility as their living room. Many come every day to meet their friends and see a bit of the activity downtown in much the same way that people traditionally gathered around village squares.

Ambience

With talented designers and plenty of money for materials the Indoor City can offer almost any environment imaginable. This is amply demonstrated in the grandiose West Edmonton Mall, which combines 600 stores with an amusement park, a triple loop roller coaster, an official NHL-size hockey rink, seven-acre water park with six-foot surf and a replica of the Santa Maria, settled in a large aquarium that visitors can explore in a submarine. Here, at first glance it appears that perfection has been reached. It's neither too cold nor hot, there is no snow or even slippery surfaces, no dogs that chase, no cars that pollute or people who are threatening. And, in a bar on "Bourbon Street," clever lighting offers a choice between a warm indoor environment and a cool terrace located under the stars.

It is here, however, that the basic problem with the ambience of the Indoor City emerges. The Indoor City, as represented by the West Edmonton Mall, is frozen in time. There are no shifting light patterns as the day progresses and no seasons. While many of the centres attached to the Indoor City try to embrace city-centre functions and provide a locus for people to meet and be involved in the hubbub of city life, they create a contrived environment that has the illusion of spontaneity but, in reality is carefully orchestrated. The organic process of city building and rebuilding that occurs through the actions of thousands of independent actors in the street environment are often sanitized beyond recognition in the indoor mega-project environment.

There are other problems with the ambience of Montreal's Indoor City. These include long, uninteresting tunnels such as that between Place Bonaventure and the Métro, poorly ventilated spaces such as the McGill Métro and noisy, odorous food courts. There are not enough places to sit and relax in most parts of the system.

Happily, there are signs of a change for the better. The flagship of the system, Place Ville Marie, has recently completed major renovations that included the creation of well-lit atriums and a much more casual seating arrangement.

Planning Issues

Currently there is a terrific amount of controversy among professionals who are debating what should be done with the Indoor City. The range of views is enormous. Some are repulsed by the private commercial nature of much of the system and are convinced that an enclosed environment will always be a very poor substitute for open-air civic space. They go so far as to suggest that the system should be dismantled. Instead, they argue, the city should use its resources to enhance open-air sidewalks, squares and parks. Others, noting the general popularity of the Indoor City, suggest that it should be extended wherever possible. Finally, there are those who argue that there are advantages to both the indoor and outdoor public environments and, with careful planning, these places can play complementary roles. These issues are well-debated in William Whyte's fascinating book, entitled *City*.

Large multipurpose centres such as Complexe Desjardins or St. Catherine Street's new shopping malls are at the heart of this controversy. While these centres can do a great deal to revitalize an ailing city core, they also extract a price. The best way for a city to meet the economic and social responsibilities associated with its retail development is to ensure that there is a balance between the indoor and on-street environment. With due care these environments can be mutually reinforcing. There is no substitute for on-street retail stores in good weather and especially during a hot summer night. On the other hand, the Indoor City is attractive during inclement weather and for people with limited mobility. Together, these facilities can contribute to a strong central business district, which is seen as an exciting place to be at all times.

In seeking an appropriate balance, the City of Montreal should give consideration to the following planning guidelines:

1. *Designate Indoor Public Space*

The city should designate primary corridors and certain open areas within the Indoor City as public space. In these areas the rules governing access and behaviour should be consistent with those in force in streets and parks. In meeting this objective the city would assume responsibility for the amenities, security, safety and maintenance of these areas. Although costly, this step is not without precedent — privately maintained toll roads were nationalized some time ago.

2. *Plan for a Variety of Experiences*

Currently, the different types of indoor environment are not well dispersed throughout the system. The centres that offer the best public amenities, Complexe Desjardins and Complexe Guy Favreau, are in close proximity. More care needs to be taken to ensure that a variety of commercial and recreational activities are available throughout the system. This is not to say that every centre should follow the same model. On the contrary, following the delightful example of the Métro, each centre should have a distinctive design.

3. *Improve Orientation*

The difficulty that people have navigating the Indoor City is legendary. This problem is obvious even to those who have tried to follow the walking tour of "Underground Montreal" described in the official tourist guide. Signs in each part of the system reflect the interests of each centre, and it is necessary to follow signs for Information, Boutiques, Passage or the name of an adjacent building to select an appropriate corridor. As most connections involve one or more shifts in level it is easy to become confused. Consistent signs identifying the main corridors that form part of the network and comprehensive maps would help. A symbol, such as the Métro sign, which is readily recognizable, yet not overbearing, is needed to indicate paths.

Orientation would also be greatly improved if it were possible to see through to the street in more locations. While such views are provided on a grand scale in Complexe Desjardins, Place Guy Favreau and Place Montréal Trust, most centres offer very little help with orientation with respect to the street network.

4. *Improve the Ambience*

The single best way to improve the ambience of the system is to allow natural light penetration wherever possible. A wonderful opportunity to provide a skylight for McGill Métro was lost with the construction of Place de la Cathédrale. Instead, we are offered a vast artificially lit catacomb. Sound and smell are also concerns in some parts of the system. Clearly, more care should be taken in the design of food courts.

5. *Provide Public Amenities*

Seats, foliage, fountains, washrooms and other amenities indicate that a centre is welcoming to the general public. Moveable chairs and tables, such as those recently installed following major renovations to the Place Ville Marie concourse, are greatly preferred to the rigid, stationary benches in most centres. These avoid creating a "gauntlet of eyes" watching passersby and allow natural groups to form around a table.

6. *Improve Access for the Handicapped*

The Indoor City is a terrific boom for the handicapped and others who have limited mobility. However, access is severely restricted to several parts of the system, including the Métro, the public facility that forms the backbone of the system. The availability of a special bus service for handicapped people is poor compensation for the freedom many would feel if they had full access to the network.

7. *Improve Links with the Street*

The ease of transition between the Indoor City and the street is the key element in ensuring that they play a complementary role in the vitality of the city. Entrances should be frequent and clearly marked, with stores located in centres along a retail artery having direct access to the street. Blank walls, the symbol of suburban shopping centres everywhere, are completely inappropriate in the downtown setting. The street should remain the main retail level and a primary concern in the design of new buildings.

8. *Prepare a Plan and Planning Process*

The Indoor City has developed surprisingly well for a network without a plan. At this point, however, a plan is urgently needed to ensure that the system rectifies the problems noted above and that future extensions take into account the need to balance indoor and on-street commerce and promote the vitality of the overall downtown area. Soon, a second passage under St. Catherine will be constructed linking the new Centre Eaton with Place Ville Marie and a third is under discussion linking Les Cours Mont-Royal with the Dominion Square building, Sun Life and Place Ville Marie. Properly planned, these connections could contribute to the vitality of St. Catherine Street, but they could just as easily weaken it.

 The preparation of a plan will be informative, as basic data will have to be collected concerning the commercial structure and pedestrian movements for both the Indoor City and street environments. The plan should lead to the classification of the nodes and links that are necessary to support an appropriate public facility as well as the development of design standards for all parts of the system.

Montreal's Indoor City has the potential to soak up the vitality of the retail core, to carefully separate the ingredients and create places that have all the superficial beauty and durability of artificial plants, while the street environment, undernourished, fades. With planning and appropriate public-private collaboration, however, the benefits of the system could be realized without jeopardizing the vitality of on-street commerce and without compromising the central responsibility of a city to meet the diverse needs of all of its citizens.

Streets Can Be
A City's Living Room

DEREK DRUMMOND

In every city there is a network of public and quasi-public spaces that support, even stimulate, social encounters or pleasant personal experiences. The magnitude and extent of this network and the degree to which it is accessible to all citizens is a good measure of the liveability of that city. Central to its future liveability is the value placed on such a network by its citizens, its civic authorities and, most importantly, by those responsible for its buildings, the developers.

Montreal has traditionally been considered one of North America's most liveable cities, a reputation founded more on its active, animated and relatively safe streets than on its physical attributes. Visitors from south of the border have revelled in the discovery of a city whose centre is not totally deserted at five o'clock every day, where they can take a stroll from their hotel late at night without fear of mugging or worse.

Is Montreal's reputation in jeopardy? Do its citizens still support the value of the city's network of socially productive open spaces?

Clearly the social value of our open spaces has deteriorated and the demand for improvement in the situation has all but dissipated. The North American trend towards polarization and privatization of cities and towns is being felt in Montreal. Organized concern for the urban environment has been focused on the retention of "heritage" buildings, while many of the urban spaces that previously supported socially important activities have been removed or altered — with the distinct objective of reducing or entirely wiping out that type of activity — and all this is happening without much comment or expression of concern.

Most North American urban dwellers are far more worried about protection than with the social life in their community. Bluntly, it appears that they fear and wish to avoid people not in their own socio-economic class and seek environments to which access is controlled. There is an increasing demand for the segregation of our communities based on income level, and the income level upon which this demand arises is dropping. Far from being concerned with public life, they are insistent on protected private life — a non-threatening existence where contact with others is reduced to views from their smart, imported cars.

Compare this with life in the neighbourhoods of ethnic groups who treasure social interaction. These areas support an active street life filled with informal social interactions that are based more on chance or unplanned encounters than on organized events.

Walk through "Little Italy" in Montreal near the intersection of St. Laurent Boulevard and Dante Street or on the streets of St. Léonard and observe the street life in those predominantly Italian communities. The street or public domain is treated as common ground and essentially as a social space. Although private property is well defined and decorated, the space in front of dwelling units is treated as an outdoor living room. In fine weather, or even in just passable weather, people are sitting outside — not in the private yard at the rear, but at the front of the house where they can converse with one another and with passersby. The lack of a porch seems almost immaterial — merely an inconvenience but not a hindrance to sitting outside. The front step will suffice if necessary. Nothing that architects and home builders do can undermine this fundamental aspect of Italian lifestyle and behaviour.

Similar encounters and behaviour can be also found in other quarters of the city with large concentrations of the less affluent. Although these areas support an active street life, social interaction is based on financial circumstances, not on cultural background. Here, the activities taking place in the street are as much a result of living conditions inside the house as other influences. Crowding, small rooms and extended families force members of the family to seek refuge outside in suitable weather. As soon as they can afford to, these people move to neighbourhoods where the social activities are influenced by ethnic origin and lifestyle rather than economic means.

Other Montrealers value privacy and private space more than the informal social life associated with public space. Front yards are decorative, not social spaces. Rear yards are fenced for privacy and this is the

Bocce game is typical of the animated
activity found in parks in Montreal's
predominantly Italian St. Léonard district.
Courtesy of The Gazette.

St. Laurent Boulevard during one of its
increasingly popular street festivals.
Photo by Pierre Obendrauf, The Gazette.

Redesign of St. Catherine Street sidewalk in front
of Christ Church Cathedral to accommodate the
entrance to Place de la Cathédrale shopping centre
reduces its potential as a social space.
Photo by Bryan Demchinsky.

Below-grade entrances are common along redesigned McGill
College Avenue, leaving little usable space for seating.
Photo by David Sidaway.

outdoor space that is used. Neighbours tend to be nodding acquaintances — only casual, usually weather related conversation, is considered tactful. Social life is mainly based on organized events or associated with organizations or clubs where the participating group is controlled. Public open space has little or no role to play.

There are, of course, exceptions. The pressure of third parties can stimulate adults to enter into the type of interpersonal behaviour that some ethnic groups need no such help to engage in. Children and dogs provide the excuse most adults need to go to the municipal park and actually engage in informal, occasionally long conversations with others with similar props. The type of animated informal social interaction associated with the children's play area, or the "dog-run," however, does not occur in other sections of the park. An adult without the requisite child or dog attempting to join such groups would be treated with scorn, even fear.

As one would expect, the activities in parks in Montreal's Italian neighbourhoods are distinctive. In Little Italy, Parc Dante attracts local citizens for quiet relaxation and conversation at all times of the day. No props are necessary. In St. Léonard, Parc Ladauversière, a large park with playing fields, swimming pool, basketball courts and other recreational facilities, supports activities more akin to those expected in a Venetian campo or a Roman piazza than in a municipal park in North America. Particularly in the evening after the dinner hour, people of all ages drift toward one area of the park where they congregate. The older men play cards, the middle-aged play bocce and teenagers, at least in the summer, play basketball. There are always more spectators than players — spectators involved in excited comments on the games or in animated conversation among themselves or even with the players. The park is a marvellous refuge for all members of the community, particularly for the elderly.

Within the Italian community, there are streets with shops and restaurants with a distinctive Italian flavour — not unlike the parks mentioned above. These shopping streets attract similar gatherings of people of all ages — sometimes grouped around a lone bench, often in the middle of the sidewalk — but always locked in animated and prolonged discussion.

Unlike the behaviour in parks, this type of interaction does occur on shopping streets and elsewhere in the city, but with less intensity and with fewer people involved. The vast majority of Montrealers need props, specific areas or situations for this type of activity.

The potential for an extensive network of public spaces suitable is tremendous, but for a number of reasons little advantage is taken of it. The objective should be clear: to create suitable conditions for pedestrians to stop, to stand, to sit, to rest, to sunbathe, to people-watch and even to chat. Such places are fundamental to our enjoyment of urban life. But investigate any part of our city and it will be discovered that there are surprisingly few such places, and their number is decreasing.

Public spaces occur in all parts of the city, but they are most important in shopping areas where large numbers of people are concentrated. Here, the greatest potential source of such places — our sidewalks — is treated as second-class space by planners and civic authorities. It is the space left over after the street has been designed for vehicular traffic. We need only observe St. Catherine Street, Montreal's busiest pedestrian street, where instead of widening the overcrowded sidewalks, parking places have been provided — an indication of civic priorities.

To expand the network of places to stop or to sit in public, the city should widen all sidewalks by five feet, thus removing one lane of traffic or one row of parking. The extra width could be used for planting trees and installing benches. Since people like to watch the passing scene, these benches should be placed with their backs at the inside edge of the sidewalk against a building, if one exists. If the street is too narrow to allow expansion of both sidewalks, consideration should be given to widening the sidewalk on the sunny side of the street only.

The design of plazas in front of office buildings and city squares should be modified to provide seating in accordance with suggestions resulting from the research done by William Whyte in New York and Jan Gehl in Denmark and others. They discovered where citizens prefer to sit in squares and plazas, namely at the edge of the plaza or square facing the sidewalk and street. There is absolutely no desire to sit in the middle of the space.

Hence it is the design of edges — that space immediately bordering the sidewalk — that is so critical to the network of public spaces. It is here that the designer or developer makes a conscious decision whether to attract or to discourage social activities, whether to invite people to stop or to encourage them to just pass by. The recent trend is definitely toward the latter and we must find ways to change the situation.

Some of the most successful seating areas at the sidewalk edge were designed for other purposes. Monumental steps, such as those at the entrance to the Montreal Museum of Fine Arts, provide excellent seating, almost a grandstand from which to observe the street. Traditional building design dictated that for any important structure, the entrance be above the level of the sidewalk and be reached by a significant set of steps. The more important the building, the more impressive the stairway. There are a number of these potential grandstands in the older parts of our cities, which in suitable weather provide ideal seating.

Unfortunately, in recent years, the custom has been to place the building entry below the level of the sidewalk, making necessary steps that drop down from the sidewalk, orienting the grandstand toward the building. An example is 2001 University, at the corner of University St. and de Maisonneuve Boulevard. Developers are attracted to sunken steps because according to a zoning bylaw, any area below the mean ground level of the site does not count in the calculations determining the allowable buildable area of the project, and therefore the entry level becomes a bonus.

This provision in the bylaw must be altered if we wish to avoid the streetscapes such as that found on McGill College Avenue, where virtually all buildings take advantage of the provision with the result being little usable — not to mention inviting — seating along the entire length of the street. One suspects, in this case, that there also is a deliberate attempt by developers to discourage seating since they cannot control the users of these quasi-public spaces. "Undesirables" sitting on plazas of "prestige" office towers send tremors of fear into the hearts of developers, although the undesirables are no more undesirable than the office towers are prestigious.

Buildings situated without a set-back from the sidewalk present different opportunities. Even in these cases, the designer can create small but enormously important urban spaces. The mere provision of one six-inch step above the sidewalk to a ledge on which a person can stand, facing but safely apart from the pedestrian traffic, will attract people watchers. If the ledge is exposed to the sun and protected from the wind, so much the better. Such ledges do occur along St. Catherine Street, the most successful being in front of the Bank of Nova Scotia just west of Peel on the north side. For years, this vantage point has provided (particularly for the lunch-time crowd) a perch from which to observe the passing pedestrian traffic — a commercial version of the residential front porch.

More often than not these ledges were not intended as benches, and it is not uncommon for them to be altered in such a way as to make sitting difficult if not impossible. Uncomfortable textured metal or masonry surfaces are added, apparently to prevent the very activities we should, as a city, be trying to promote.

Christ Church Cathedral, in the redesign of its St. Catherine Street edge to accommodate entrances to the new shopping centre entombed in its former crypt, vastly reduced the potential of the edge as a social space. For years that particular section of St. Catherine Street was a socially vibrant space with the cathedral's low retaining wall and upwardly sloping lawn providing a convenient and comfortable grandstand. The sale of crafts was tolerated, and in general this activity, stimulated by the physical design of the space, contributed to life on the street. The redesign cleverly eliminates the possibility of vending or at least makes it extremely difficult. The wide steps leading to the front door of the cathedral will no doubt attract some people, but not on the previous scale.

These few examples indicate a trend away from the provision of social spaces in new buildings. Given the competitive nature of development today and the marketing strategies for new projects based on well-defined "target groups," the exclusivity of quasi-public spaces or edges will continue to grow. Only social controls in the form of bylaws, or a mandatory project review that encourages a more humane approach to the design of the quasi-public realm will redirect this trend.

The authorities have the power to promote widening of sidewalks and redesign of public squares, and to mandate changes in bylaws controlling developers' actions. So far they have been reluctant to exercise this power except in a few isolated cases.

One such initiative has been the attempt over the years to investigate the viability of creating a number of pedestrian malls. An inner city response to the threat of the popular suburban shopping centres of the 1960s, the pedestrian mall was believed a saviour. By eliminating auto traffic from the street, it was felt that shoppers would be attracted back into the city because they could walk freely between shops on either side of the street as they do in a shopping centre. An attempt to create a permanent mall on Mount Royal Avenue between Chambord and Marquette Streets (just west of Papineau) in 1970 was disastrous; it only lasted a few weeks. Proposals for vehicle-free streets have been experimented with on Prince Arthur, Duluth, Crescent Street and others.

Difficulties arise not so much from the effect on the street itself but from the impact on the immediate neighbourhood. Prince Arthur, for example, has become a regional restaurant centre serving a large portion of the city — it is anything but a neighbourhood shopping street. The impact, on the other hand, of thousands of Montrealers in search of Italian, Greek or Vietnamese food in the neighbourhood is devastating. The urban ecology is fragile and can only be altered with extreme care. Permanent pedestrian malls can be socially destructive rather than positive additions to the public life of the city.

Temporary malls, which close a street to auto traffic for a day or at most a week for sidewalk sales or community related events, can be socially productive as well as commercially successful. The impact on the immediate surrounding neighbourhood can be severe but only for a short period of time. The odds are that most people in the neighbourhood will join in the activity and benefit from the event.

After studying these types of events, from sidewalk sales to Portuguese festivals with their neighbourhood processions, I am still amazed at the extent of the delight expressed by people participating in one way or another. Individual behavioural patterns are altered, at least for a day. Shopping becomes a social experience — strangers talk to one another. It's as though some hidden drive for a public social life is temporarily revealed and allowed to blossom.

We should consider the market place rather than a shopping mall as a model for the city and as an appropriate guide to decision-making. Although our city centres are fast becoming shopping zones modelled on the great regional shopping malls of the suburbs — manipulative, crassly commercial, controlled, exclusive, homogenized environments from which the all important network of public social spaces is slowly being eliminated, the model for a more humane and liveable city is nevertheless close at hand. The ambience of the Jean Talon or Atwater markets or even Le Faubourg downtown should provoke us to considering the city as something more than a commercial development dominated by large, powerful corporations. The energy and chaos, the lack of storefronts, narrow paths, goods displayed without plastic containers, the sights and smells of the market place and the sound of voices in conversation appeals to me, and I am sure, to many others, more than muzak and the almost pristine world of the mall.

A commitment to a more humane, liveable city, perhaps at the expense of some perceived efficiencies and conveniences, must be made. A giant step forward would be the extension of the network of public and quasi-public spaces associated with informal social and personal activities that can and should take place in our urban spaces. Present trends must be assessed and new initiatives undertaken. The city's reputation will be enhanced and its citizens will be the richer for such actions.

The Fine Art of Enhancing Public Places

ALINE GUBBAY

In 1892, the sculptor Philippe Hebért returned to Montreal from his Paris studio to inspect the proposed site for his monument to Paul de Chomedey Sieur de Maisonneuve, Montreal's founder. He declared the location, in Place d'Armes, suitably historic and the assigned space adequate. Hebért was much less complimentary on the state of public art to be found in the city which, he said, lagged sadly behind the cities of Europe. There, a long tradition of state sponsorship of the arts had embellished the squares, plazas, parks and public buildings with an outdoor feast of artistic display.

The number of Montreal's public sculptures at the time numbered just two. Nelson's column on Notre Dame Street was erected in 1809, funded by public subscription in an emotional outburst following the news of Nelson's death at Trafalgar. More than 60 years later a statue to Queen Victoria was unveiled, in 1872, in the old Haymarket Square, now renamed in the queen's honour. The occasion was marked by a public holiday. The governor-general, the Marquess of Dufferin, made a graceful bilingual speech, and the celebrations continued with a ball at which the marquess danced all night "never flagging till four in the morning."

There were celebrations of another kind for the unveiling of the de Maisonneuve monument some 20 years later. The first major monument in the city to a Canadian by a Canadian-born sculptor, it released a storm of emotion and widespread civic pride. Place d'Armes was hung with shields and banners, there was a good deal of music, singing and dancing and a great many speeches. The monument quickly became the city's most recognizable symbol. People who had never been inside a museum or art gallery felt free to comment on the artistic merits of the sculpture (the reaction was overwhelmingly favourable) and a lot of them wondered why it had taken so long to achieve.

The truth was, as it continues to be, that placing a work of art in a public place is a hazardous, frustrating, controversial and complicated process. It requires the co-operation of municipal, and possibly provincial, councils (what is the benefit to the city in this project?), influential citizens (why should we give money for art, where is the return?), and the artist (how can I be expected to turn out a reasonable piece for little money?). Even given the widespread enthusiasm among the general public for the de Maisonneuve monument, there were at the time grave misgivings as to the cost.

The artist initially chosen for the project when it was first proposed in the 1870s was Napoléon Bourassa. His design — de Maisonneuve as a mediaeval knight above a screen of falling water ornamented with beavers — was greatly admired and the use of the beavers praised for adding a nice Canadian touch. Best of all, wrote the *Canadian Illustrated News*, "Mr. Bourassa is wealthy and needs no compensation beyond what is required for the material outlay."

This must have come as news to the artist, but in the event the undertaking required another 20 years of persistence on the part of a committee of devoted amateur historians, years of endless meetings with city council, with community groups and with influential financiers. When the project was finally realized, it was with a totally new sculpture, by a new artist, Bourassa's pupil, Philippe Hebért.

How has Montreal fared in the hundred years since the saga of the de Maisonneuve monument? The basic problems remain very much in place. Cooperation between groups is still essential, though the emphasis shifts with the movement of financial responsibility from the public to the private sector. The fundamental questions remain: why do we need public art, how does it add to the quality of urban life, and will more important needs be shortchanged if we spend money on these "extras?"

It is tempting to reply simply that we need art in our lives more than ever, now that so many of us are isolated from daily social exchange by our cars, TV sets, Walkmans, high-rise apartments or suburban homes; that the arts are as necessary to our survival as human beings as the air we breathe.

The Maisonneuve monument in Place d'Armes
is an early example of public art in Montreal.
Photo by Len Sidaway, The Gazette.

The 'Homage to Jackie Robinson' has been moved to a more appropriate site next to the Olympic stadium.
Photo by Aline Gubbay.

However, if we think of art only as the paintings, sculpture and delicate decorative arts stored or displayed in our museums, it is obvious these reach, touch and influence only a fraction of the population. It is the function of art in public places to bring the joy, stimulation, controversy and general affirmation of life that art provides, out into the streets where we can all see it — on our way to work, strolling about when we have the leisure, or as the main objective of an outing. There are no barriers between us and public works of art. They allow us to exercise our judgment, to admire or disapprove, to be shocked or to laugh, and perhaps, over time, to come to understand where before we were puzzled, to appreciate where initially we scoffed.

International events in Montreal produced an outburst of public display that included numerous works of art. In the festive atmosphere generated by such events, numbers of visitors experienced their first exposure to art, absorbing, perhaps unconsciously, the pleasurable stimulation to the senses it provides. As a legacy of these festivals we have, for example, from Expo 67, Alexander Calder's giant "Running Man" and Buckminster Fuller's glorious bubble, which in its breathtaking elegance must qualify as a work of art. The Métro stations finished in time for the Olympics of 1976 house some of the most striking art throughout the system, and Jean-Paul Riopelle's fountain, on the plaza leading to the Olympic Stadium, is a joyous and humorous creation that deserves to be better known.

In the general run of events, public art has been and continues to be dominated by sculpture of two kinds: one is commemorative and the other unrelated to specific people and events. Into the first category fall the war memorials and cenotaphs, the statues to politicians, prelates and individuals who have achieved distinction in their fields. These put us in touch with history, local or worldwide. Most are monuments financed in large part by governments. Others come about through a grass-roots surge of spontaneous enthusiasm for a folk hero, someone not easily classifiable as an important or venerable personage.

Some memorable monuments of this type have appeared on the streets of Montreal during the past 20 years. In the heart of the district from which he came stands Louis Cyr, the famous son of a Ste. Cunégonde policeman who became an international strong man and weight-lifting champion. He is placed in a traditional setting, a vest-pocket park with benches so that one may sit and admire this splendid work. Also traditional is the pedestal upon which Louis Cyr stands, and his posture, head up, arms crossed, a pose remarkable similar to that of businessman John Young in Philippe Hebért's statue of him on the waterfront. The stance, however, is warmed and humanized in Robert Pelletier's sculpture by his portrayal of Cyr's powerful, muscular frame, clothed in old-fashioned athletic clothing.

Louis Cyr's monument is well known and well loved in spite of its comparatively obscure location at the corner of St. Jacques and Coursol Streets. Since its appearance in 1970 our times have become increasingly wary of heroes. We are more comfortable finding flaws in, rather than in looking up to the achievers in our society. This has led to a marked change in the design of the memorials with a move to bringing the individual closer to the viewer. Even a revered figure like Brother André, originally placed on a modestly high pedestal close to St. Joseph's Oratory, now stands on a low, rough rock, close to the ground, in the little urban green space renamed for him at the busy corner of René Lévesque Boulevard and Beaver Hall Hill.

The memorial to Jackie Robinson brings the baseball legend who began his professional career in Montreal, literally down to earth. He is shown looking down into the adoring faces of two small children. All three stand flat on the ground, their feet partly hidden in the dirt. Ranged in a short curve before them are short rows of bleachers, seats on which one may sit to view the group. However, unlike the spectator role played by a viewer from a park bench, we are invited here to assume a role in the ensemble, to become an active component in the concept. The Robinson memorial, like that of Louis Cyr, was originally placed close to the scene of his association with Montreal, the Delorimier baseball grounds where the Montreal Royals played. But while historically correct as a location, it proved too isolated from a busy pedestrian flow and the group has now been moved to the Olympic Stadium where it provides a sense of continuity with Montreal baseball's new home.

This new intimacy, which encourages interaction between an artist's work and the public, is found now in many examples of non-commemorative sculpture. Since these tend to be privately owned and occasionally privately commissioned, they are scattered, like items in a treasure hunt, up and down the city streets and open spaces — a Barbara Hepworth on the McGill campus, a Henry Moore across from Dominion Square, an Etrog on Sherbrooke Street.

Among the pioneers in making works of art accessible to the public was the late Max Stern. The magnificent Rodin figure from the

"Burghers of Calais" group, set on the Sherbrooke Street sidewalk in front of Stern's Dominion Gallery, was for many their first encounter with a major work of art. It is worth recalling that Rodin himself had wanted the figures in this group to be placed, not on a raised podium, which is what the city fathers of Calais insisted upon, but single file at ground level where the public would encounter them face to face. More recent works on public view include J. Seward Johnson's "Catching Up," the relaxed figure of a man reading a newspaper as he casually leans against the entry door to an office building on Sherbrooke Street. This work has intrigued and delighted countless people whose image of public art was of something vastly more remote and inaccessible.

Lea Vivot's "Lovers' Bench" of 1979, with its nude figures, two of whom are found in an embrace, stirred a good deal of public controversy as it intrigued, shocked and amused passersby. It now sits, more or less sedately, in the bucolic surroundings of the Botanical Gardens in Maisonneuve Park. Her current work, on display on McGill College Avenue, is far less controversial. "The Secret Bench — Lost Paradise" has two youngsters seated close together at one end of a park bench. Pedestrians often stop, look, and sit alongside, creating a living, changing tableau. The work proved so popular that after an initial trial period it has been bought by a consortium of companies in the immediate area.

There is plenty of interaction between works of art and the public across the street. Raymond Mason's haunting, disturbing "Illuminated Crowd" is hardly lovable but its power cannot leave the onlooker unmoved. "I am a narrative artist," Mason has said, "like Hogarth or Rowlandson. I try to portray the range of the human comedy — humour, hope, fear, sickness, violence, death." The range is there for all to unravel in his crowded group, caught in the glare of a searchlight or the headlights of a car. This is a challenging work, commissioned by the Dreyfus Group of the Banque Nationale de Paris. Backed by the deep blue of the building's glass curtain wall, the yellow polyester-resin sculpture arrests the eye and cannot be ignored.

Not many patrons are willing to sponsor as controversial a piece of public art as the "Illuminated Crowd." Most developers of the huge new office blocks jostling for space in the McGill College-de Maisonneuve-Sherbrooke sector have attempted to humanize their buildings with landscaping, which sometimes incorporates a work of sculpture. Ron Williams's sensitively scaled and graded design for the plaza stretching the length of the Industrial Life Tower on McGill College, includes plants, trees, seating, a fountain and a sculpture — "Danseuse" by Zoya Niederman, which was specifically chosen by Eugene Riesman, head of First Quebec Corporation, developer of the Industrial Life Tower.

Around the corner on Sherbrooke Street, the otherwise undistinguished Central Trust building is graced with a polished little plaza housing the most elegant sculpture on display in the streets of Montreal, Barry Flanagan's "Kouros Horse." J. Kracauer of J.K. Investments is the patron of this harmonious ensemble, the plaza having been designed by his architect son.

There is a desperate need for more plazas and green and open spaces among the forest of high-rise towers in the downtown core. Maison Alcan on Sherbrooke Street is in this regard a shining beacon, community-oriented, with its small, beautifully detailed parks tucked between the project's various component parts, none of which rises above eight storeys in height. Its atrium has also become a model for other such city spaces with its innovative arts program. This includes playing host to a number of varied works — reliefs, wall hangings and magnificent specimens of Inuit sculpture. Among the recent additions to its collection is a large-scale bronze, by Esther Wertheimer, of the doomed lovers Paolo and Francesca, a dramatic work given sympathetic background space in the soaring volume of the atrium.

An outstanding example of the integration of art in public places over the past 20 years is Montreal's Métro. From the outset, when construction began in 1962, the decision was taken to emphasis variety in station design. Private architectural firms, as well as those working exclusively for the city, were each assigned to one of the 26 stations planned. Architects were given free reign in their designs, but were instructed to include adequate space for the works of art which, it was hoped, would follow in due course. Since the architects had no way of knowing which artists would be chosen, or what form their work might take, the space usually set aside for them was an expanse of wall at some level of the ensemble.

Stained glass, used with great ingenuity, emerged as a favoured and flexible material. The pioneer in its large-scale use in the stations was Marcelle Ferron. Her vivid windows, with their soaring, abstract designs for Champ de Mars station, remain among the most striking examples of all Métro art. Stained glass also lends itself well to narrative content, and designs were adapted to reflect a particular station's geographical

'Kouros Horse' is an elegant addition to the plaza
of the Central Trust building on Sherbrooke Street.
Photo by Aline Gubbay.

'Catching Up' features a man reading a newspaper near
the entrance to a Sherbrooke Street office building.
Photo by Aline Gubbay.

Brother André in his new home
near the top of Beaver Hall Hill.
Photo by Aline Gubbay.

'The Illuminated Crowd' makes a bold statement outside
the Banque Nationale de Paris on McGill College Avenue.
Photo by Aline Gubbay.

location or events identified with its name. Frederic Back's mural of the history of music in Montreal, found an appropriate setting on the mezzanine level at Place des Arts. A great mural located on the platform level at McGill station, by Nicolas Sollogoub, draws on Montreal history of the period 1800–1870, and is centred with portraits of Jacques Viger, the city's first mayor and his successor Peter McGill. Jean Cartier's glass mural at Papineau station also takes its theme from the station's name. It commemorates the Patriotes rebellion of 1837–38 and is dedicated to one of its leaders, Louis-Joseph Papineau.

But lack of patrons meant that many stations were left bare of decoration beyond that incorporated by the architects in their overall design. Then in 1970, along with the creation of the Montreal Urban Community, a new entity, the Bureau de Transport Métropolitain (BTM) was given sole charge of the Métro and its planned expansion, with a clear mandate to establish its own norms, priorities and directives. The board soon announced that the policy of assigning each station to a different architect remained in place but with an important difference. Architects were now asked to integrate works of art in their initial design. They were free to choose their artists but were required to work with them from the outset. It was to be a co-operative effort, artist and architect working together to produce the finished unit. The BTM also undertook to pay the artists directly. The search for donors was over and the BTM became a patron of the arts on a scale unknown before in Montreal.

Under this new regime, 39 more stations have been added to the Métro system in the period 1970–1988. While results may be judged uneven, all are intriguing. The major difference has come from the variety of forms, materials and subject matter now on display. Architects have been able to incorporate spaces for sculptures, murals and mobiles at many station levels. Colourful shapes which harmonized the artists' and architects' concepts could be designed as part of the basic structural necessities.

This partnership idea did not always work, and some architects decided to act as their own artists in order to be able carry through their own concepts, unhindered by having to accommodate another artist's ideas. This has sometimes worked well as, for example, in the Edouard Montpetit station where the architect has carried forward the elegant detail of the outside walls into the entrance and on to the platforms in a variety of modifications.

In other instances the new working arrangement between artist and architect has given us results impossible under the old system. For example, Peter Gnass's glorious mobile at LaSalle station has been provided with all the space it needs for its soaring display. Similarly, Gérmain Bergeron's stylized figures, at Monk, so spare in line but occupying volumes of space, are seen in a setting that gives them great impact and drama.

There is a broad range of styles on view. Some stations are entirely abstract in design. Some incorporate exterior views as their contribution to the station's decor. Others include specific references in their murals and furniture — benches, lamps, etc. — to the built environment on the streets outside, as at Outremont and de Castelnau.

How much of this artistic feast is enjoyed by the Métro's passengers? It is surely no exaggeration to say that many of us have felt cheered and our spirits lightened by the colour and diversity around us. Most of us will become familiar with barely a handful of the system's 65 stations — our local stop and those at which we regularly disembark for work or leisure pursuits. Perhaps it takes a visit to New York or London's subways to shock us into recognizing the Aladdin's treasure trove provided for us by our own public utility.

At the time of writing, Montreal appeared to be on the verge of a breakthrough in the field of sponsorship of the public arts. In the public sector, the Commission d'Initiatives et Developpement Culturel (CIDEC) was due to announce a new policy in the fall of 1989, which we are told will demonstrate a bold and generous gesture in encouraging a steady increase of art in public places. Already, the province requires that one per cent of the cost of construction of a new building that receives provincial funding must be spent on art. And, also from the private sector, comes the consultant group l'Association de Promotion d'art et d'architecture de Montréal. Christophe Caron, its vice-president, reports on a vigorous campaign to involve leaders of industry and commerce in sponsorship of the arts, seen as an integral part of building design, and early information is that the reaction has been very favourable.

The forgotten component seems to be the artist. Too often artists have been persuaded to "loan" their works to decorate a plaza, lobby or entrance, with no fee offered, management assuming the advertisement value to be sufficient reward. This is a deplorable practice. If it is to continue, some fee scale should be established as rent, payable to the artist. Artists will often work for very little in order to continue in the field they love, but they must live too. Work materials are expensive and studio space is both a basic necessity and a recurring problem. A disheartening sequence has often seen artists moving into unwanted lofts or warehouses for the open workspace they provide, only to find after a time that these spaces have become fashionable and desirable as living accommodation. Rents soar and the artists must move on.

Some years back city council discussed the idea, which died stillborn, of setting up an artists' quarter where low-rent studio space would be made available to artists. Such a scheme was actually put in place in Alexandria, Virginia, in 1974. An old munitions factory, built during the First World War, was converted to an arts centre with studio and workshop space for 200 artists, four co-operative art galleries and an art school for more than 600 students. The centre has since become a thriving, integrated part of the city's life. Visitors are welcome and the old barriers between public and artist have been imaginatively and successfully bridged.

The experience of another American city provides further food for thought. When Seattle was in crisis in 1968, with the Boeing Corporation's dismissal of 64,000 of its 104,000 workers, the mayor, Wes Uhlman, invested half a million dollars of city funds a year to support struggling arts organizations of many kinds — theatre, dance, music, as well as the plastic arts. With this encouragement they survived the bad years and continue to flourish. The lesson, said Uhlman, was this: "If we support our artists and treat them with respect, they respond by enriching our city and the life of virtually every citizen."

ARCHITECTURE

Even if, as urbanist Jean-Claude Marsan has said, most architecture in Montreal is derivative, the eclecticism, the quality of production from styles developed elsewhere, and the city's building pattern, which has produced such characteristic structures as the greystones, have created an urban environment of admirable diversity.

How well has Montreal's recent architecture contributed to this legacy? As in the past, Montreal has been a follower of influences; where once neo-Gothic and neo-Classical forms gave way to Beaux-Arts, today Postmodernism attempts to shove Modernism from the stage.

Out of this ferment has come a crop of new buildings clamoring for status as significant architecture. While history will help determine which of these deserve the accolade, opinion of their worth is already in abundant supply.

Significant Buildings of the 1980s

RICARDO L. CASTRO

The state of architecture in Montreal during the past decade can be summarized by three prevalent practices: the use of an aesthetic of invisibility, a taxidermic approach to the preservation of architectural heritage and an open confrontation with the idea of architectural propriety. Montreal's significant buildings of the 1980s will undoubtedly be those that have resisted these practices.

The Invisible City

Our perception of the city has been shaped by a world increasingly dominated by media. Attention span, once conditioned to longer periods of concentration, has been fractured by television and the microchip. Now, some argue, it only lasts the time between commercials. It should not come as a surprise that reality, including our appreciation of the built environment, has acquired a fragmented presence as well.

Like the TV program, interest sustained by a piece of environment, whether good or bad, beautiful or ugly, is ephemeral. Suffice to examine architectural examples in our own urban territory. Buildings that caught the public's attention last year or the year before or even last month have been overtaken by the latest arrivals. These in turn will lose place to those just being erected.

Take, for example, the Olympic Stadium, erected for the 1976 games.

Its tower, designed to support the retractable roof, was finally completed in 1989. Thanks to our perceptual numbness the stadium was built without major opposition despite the fact that it is a conspicuous architectural eyesore as well as the most outrageous use of public funds in the city's history. On the other hand, the monumental Grain Elevator No. 1 was demolished in 1983, erasing a significant example of early industrial architecture from Montreal's waterfront.

More recently La Maison des Coopérants, topped by its distinctive Batman's hood, stirred controversy because of its sheer size, and glitzy, unorthodox use of the underground precinct of Christ Church Cathedral as another shopping mall. This project, along with several like it, occupied a prominent place in the public's attention and in critics' imagination. For their qualities or lack thereof, they were famous or infamous. But only for those fleeting 15 minutes that the late Andy Warhol claimed would constitute the time span of fame in the television age.

In his recent book *Amerique* (Paris; Bernard Grasset, 1988, pp. 196) the French sociologist and media critic Jean Baudrillard noted:

> In New York there is a double phenomenon: each of the great buildings dominates or has once dominated the city, each of the ethnic groups dominates or has, in their own way, once dominated the city. Promiscuity gives sparkle to each of the components of the city, while elsewhere it tends to abolish the differences. In Montreal all the components exist — the ethnic groups, the buildings, the North American space — but without the sparkle and violence of the U.S. cities.

It is intriguing that the photograph that illustrates the cover of the original French version of Baudrillard's book is not of the New York City skyline but of Montreal's. At first there seems nothing wrong with this visual simulation in which the Hydro-Québec building, Place Ville Marie and Complex Desjardins substitute for the Empire State, Chrysler building and World Trade Centre. The book's narrative — excellent reading incidentally — provides the clue as to why Montreal appears. None of the buildings represented or cited above really matters. They are interchangeable, anonymous, now part of oblivion.

The once commanding presence of architecture in the city seems to be on the wane, due to the process of endless repetition and reiteration

Downtown from a Mount Royal lookout. A monotonous barrier of glass, steel and slick veneers obstructs the visual connection between the river and the mountain.
Photo by Bryan Demchinsky.

The preservation of just two walls of the New Sherbrooke apartment building as it is converted into part of the new annex of the Montreal Museum of Fine Arts is an example of architectural taxidermy, an often unsatisfying practice.
Photo by Richard Arless Jr., The Gazette.

of the same image, whether real — the buildings themselves — or their electronic equivalents — video images.

Baudrillard has pointed out that once a thing is repeated ad infinitum it loses its uniqueness and . . . disappears. In this light, contemporary architecture is no more. It is being exhausted in the downtown of our cities as glass and granite boxes, the trademarks of high-rise architecture of the 1980s, get built every day in a futile exercise of monotonous repetition.

Whether commercial or residential, the high-rises of the 1980s have contributed little to enhance the existing architectural qualities of Montreal. Unlike their predecessors of the 1930s or even some of the buildings belonging to the 1960s and 1970s, heroic decades in Canadian architecture, the new high-rises, endlessly veneered in thin plates of marble or granite, lack strength and presence. They are but the repetition of trite themes already exhausted.

The downtown high-rises are the creation of corporate clients, promoters, and usually large architectural firms. Trying to create unique statements, they have paradoxically promoted an aesthetic of invisibility or disappearance. Observing the city from any of the mountain lookouts corroborates this thesis. There lies the downtown core where a monotonous barrier of glass, steel and slick veneers obstructs the visual connection between river and mountain, contributing nothing to the precarious sense of place that the city exudes less and less.

Architecture as Taxidermy

A new type of ephemeral structure has become visible in the streets of Montreal in recent years. It is reminiscent of the once pervasive railroad trestles used during the 19th century to conquer topographical obstructions. Today's urban "trestles" support instead old façades. These have been salvaged to become the civic masks of large and complex projects. Their architects, urban taxidermists of sorts, keep the skin of buildings, complying with developers' demands for maximum floor rentability while providing a certified heritage front in an attempt to pacify those concerned with architectural preservation.

Urban trestles can be found all over the downtown. They support large façades of 19th-century structures along St. Jacques and St. Antoine Streets in Old Montreal where the World Trade Centre is under construction. On Sherbrooke Street, across from the Montreal Museum of Fine Arts, other trestles support the two main façades of the New Sherbrooke apartment building. They will become the new-old façades of the western part of the controversial extension to the museum. These examples, and the soon-to-come conversion of the Royal George apartments on Bishop Street to a new library for Concordia University, continue the extensive practice of masking the banal and mediocre.

Despite the taxidermic interventions that have characterized some of the "preservation" work in the city during the past 10 years, some successful efforts to preserve the built heritage have taken place. As architect Joe Baker pointed out (*Canadian Architect*, November, 1988) most of these efforts have concentrated on 18th and 19th-century religious architecture, of which the city possesses abundant examples. Convents have provided an excellent source of space which has been reconditioned to fit and serve diverse functions and clients. Recycling projects have ranged from educational institutions to housing. Suffice to think of the successful rehabilitation of the Couvent du Bon Pasteur on Sherbrooke Street, the recycling into condominiums of the College Mont St. Louis also on Sherbrooke and the questionable recycling of J. Omer Marchand's significant piece of Beaux Arts architecture, the Motherhouse of the Congrégation de Notre Dame on Atwater and Sherbrooke, into Dawson College's new campus.

Industrial and commercial architecture from the last century has been recycled with various degrees of success. At the top of the list are the recycling of the Johnson & Johnson company in the Maisonneuve neighbourhood, the Berkeley Hotel as part of Maison Alcan and the conversion of the Cours Le Royer by Desnoyers Mercure into a residential and commercial complex in Old Montreal.

The recent recycling of the Mount Royal hotel into a multi-use complex raises some important issues. Gone is the great lobby that contributed so much of the old hotel's character. That space has been replaced by atriums several storeys high. Each of the levels acquires a high-gloss treatment as one moves upwards from the Métro level, where eateries, a cinema and more prosaic stores are found, to the upper storeys of the shopping concourse where the most prestigious boutiques have niches. On top of these, a nest of affluent condominiums has taken the place of the former rooms and suites of the hotel.

More acceptable is the recycling of an old garage and auto showroom on St. Catherine Street near Guy Street into Le Faubourg, a real people

The Maison des Coopérants complex on McGill College, seen here while its shopping concourse was being built under Christ Church Cathedral, was in the spotlight when it was completed in 1988.
Photo by Gordon Beck, The Gazette.

place. Here one finds a good example of an integrated or alternative mall. The formula has its precedent in the famous Faneuil Hall in Boston, rehabilitated in the 1970s. Le Faubourg houses cinemas, boutiques and shops. Merchandise is openly displayed and presented as in a bazaar. Le Faubourg may not be an extraordinary building in architectural terms. It is not the result of revolutionary concepts, yet it attracts great numbers of people. It is an easily identifiable piece of architecture, which has a definite sense of place, unlike many high-gloss competitors such as the mall in Place Montréal Trust.

Another example is architect Dan Hanganu's recycling of a multistorey garage in Outremont, now known as Le Clos St-Bernard. Here, the old structure was converted into a multi-purpose building, its silhouette modified by the addition of four two-storey penthouses. The architect opted for a design that drew inspiration from the existing building and, to an extent, from its original use. Design clues were also picked from neighbouring buildings without falling into the nostalgic manipulation of forms so often used in today's Postmodern buildings.

A Lack of Propriety

The principles of the Roman architect Vitruvius, "Firmitas, Venustas and Commoditas" (structure, beauty and function), which have guided architectural practice for more than 2,000 years, are still valid and strong. There is no question that significant buildings of our era have been designed by following the Vitruvian precepts. Less known is another principle, also coined by Vitruvius but not observed as widely: propriety.

Simply put, propriety is appropriateness, the condition that usually restrains people from wearing tuxedos to the beach or a bikini to a grand gala opening. How relevant a concept for the 1980s when much architecture could be described as lacking propriety.

For Vitruvius, propriety is the perfection of style that comes when a work is authoritatively constructed on approved principles. Accordingly, propriety can be deduced from prescription, usage or nature. In the first instance, Vitruvius gives the examples of temples open to the sky such as those dedicated to Jupiter, heaven, the moon or the sun. From usage arise other aspects of propriety: buildings with magnificent interiors that are provided with correspondingly elegant court entrances.

According to him, it would be inappropriate to access such buildings by means of low entrances. Finally, from nature come other aspects of propriety, lighting for instance. Vitruvius reminds us to light galleries and other places where a steady illumination is needed by using a northern light.

Propriety is an elusive quality of architecture, and it is not surprising that it is seldom addressed. However it is a vital quality. Propriety seemingly means to use common sense in a holistic way. Common sense undoubtedly means an appropriate use of funds, whether by private clients or taxpayers. Common sense also implies the appropriate use of materials and technology. Finally, it dictates that whatever is to be erected should improve and enhance what already exists; this is not achieved in terms of size or sensationalism as reflected by the recently built towers and malls in the core of the city.

The last decade has witnessed the erection of a vast number of projects at various scales to fulfill diverse needs. Of these, only a few can definitely boast the title of true architecture in Vitruvian terms.

During the 1980s, true architecture has been produced as a result of committed clients, and architects inclined to create quality before anything. Examples are Maison Alcan (discussed in detail elsewhere in this book), the Canadian headquarters of Johnson & Johnson Inc. and the recently completed Canadian Centre for Architecture (CCA).

Unlike most corporate headquarters with their bombastic downtown high-rises, the health-care products company Johnson & Johnson chose to remain in the Maisonneuve neighbourhood in east-end Montreal, where the company had been established in 1919. Maisonneuve is best known for the looming presence of the Olympic Stadium, but the real significance of the area lies in its history. It was here that major industrial and architectural as well as planning developments took place between the turn of the century and the beginning of World War II.

The architectural firm of Cayouette and Saïa successfully introduced a sense of history and continuity in designing a new complex for Johnson & Johnson in 1985, first by preserving and recycling some of the site's original industrial buildings and by introducing an organization of form and space that respects the Beaux Arts architectural and planning tradition found in the area.

Meanwhile, no other building in the history of the city has been so meticulously designed, built, recorded and illustrated as the Canadian Centre for Architecture. It is an austere, clear, controversial piece of

Architect Peter Rose's Canadian Centre for Architecture is a clear, controversial piece of architecture whose symbolism and precedents are thoroughly explored.
Photo by Yves Eigenmann, Canadian Centre for Architecture.

The Johnson & Johnson Inc. headquarters respects the Beaux-Arts tradition found in the Maisonneuve district.
Photo by A.D. Corsillo.

architecture that wraps around the Shaughnessy House, a heritage building from the last century.

Symbolism and precedents are thoroughly explored. For instance, the Baile Street façade is subtly broken at the middle by a vertical slit. It is a symbolic architectural gesture that acknowledges the trace of the original cadastral line that once divided the property north to south and on which the mitoyen wall of the Shaughnessy house on the opposite side rests (the Shaughnessy house was originally two semi-detached houses). The building responds in more than one way to the tacit presence of the urban grid characteristic of 17th-century French territorial organization that subsequently determined the organization of Montreal's form.

The building presents itself to the visitor as an architectural jewel whose parts are carefully assembled, each maintaining its integrity. Metal, stone, glass and wood are artfully related. By differentiating specific parts of the room and its furnishings through the use of commonly available, almost prosaic materials, splendid spaces have been created.

The CCA exemplifies how symbolism and precedents can be thoroughly explored in architecture. The building also demonstrates that significant architecture is ultimately the result of a process of differentiation that takes place at many levels, ranging from the ecological to the symbolic. The austere exterior is in context with its surroundings while the interior is sober, functional, skillfully executed and powerfully evocative. Throughout, technology is deployed, but skillfully concealed. The CCA closes the decade of the 1980s in Montreal's architecture, but that will continue to provide many readings, interpretations and critical reflections in the years to come.

However, the CCA and other good projects discussed here are exceptions rather than the norm. Looking back critically at the architecture of Montreal in the past decade, one is bound to be disappointed. Architecture has been relegated to a second plane since most of what has been built during the period unfortunately cannot be rated as other than mediocre. The sad conclusion is that the 1980s will have to be considered a "grey" decade, during which the significant buildings, the ones enhancing our memory of the city, will be those few that subscribe to the principle of propriety and point the way to an architectural method for the future.

The Decade of the Designer Tower

DEREK DRUMMOND

For more than a hundred years, architectural critics have used analogies to illustrate their ideas and to clarify the principles behind new directions in architectural design. In searching for rational explanations for both the creative process and architectural expression, linguistic, mechanical, legalistic, biological, and even gastronomical analogies have been explored. For example, as the late Peter Collins, the eminent architectural historian and connoisseur of analogies, pointed out, architecture, like gastronomy, requires intuition, imagination, enthusiasm, and an immense amount of organizational skill, as well as involving a lengthy preparation time and rich ingredients. None of these analogies, however, perhaps least of all the last one, is equal to the task of explaining the development of Montreal's office towers in the decade of the developer.

The time is ripe for a new analogy, one which not only sheds a degree of light on the trends of the last decade, but also captures the mood of a period of transition in Montreal — the transition that has seen the developer wrestle control of the decision-making process in the design of office towers from the hands of the architect.

The need for a new analogy was never before more apparent than when the plans for Place Canada Trust, the tower on the northeast corner of de Maisonneuve Boulevard and Metcalfe Street, was unveiled to the public. The initial message gleaned from studying renderings of the building is that of a conventional glass-skinned shaft being tantalizingly exposed as an outer layer of granite is peeled away — a half-peeled glass banana with granite skin. What we were witnessing was an architectural striptease. And the only way to describe it was burlesque.

Burlesque, a theatrical performance which pokes fun at an idea to the point of mockery, or which ridicules serious subjects or treats unimportant ones with false grandeur, would seem to be a singularly appropriate analogical model upon which to base a study of the principles behind the latest trend in architectural expression. It is unfortunate that the form of burlesque which springs most immediately to mind when contemplating the future Place Canada Trust is that of the vulgar variety show — the kind which features a comic striptease.

Perhaps this design is the logical conclusion of a cosmetic fad which started in the early 1980s: in stone-faced buildings, certain portions of the stone were omitted to reveal the inner glazed body of the building. Paul Goldberger, architectural critic for the *New York Times*, referred to this generation as having façades in which sections of stone look as if they were pasted on glass.

No one, to my knowledge, has taken this idea as far as the designer of Place Canada Trust. The compositional strategy of solid base and articulated shaft topped by a distinctive cap has been altered by allowing its Mussolini-Classical base to creep half-way up the curtain-walled shaft to the ninth floor. The resulting schizophrenic play between the pseudo-classical and the clinical-modern imagery is pure burlesque — the mockery of both approaches through association with their opposites. As satirical verse or burlesque, the comparison would be amusing or even stimulating. But as a piece of meaningful architecture, it is difficult to take seriously.

The well-crafted curtain-walled portion of the shaft with its reflective blue-grey glazing is probably going to remind viewers of the Banque Nationale de Paris on McGill College Avenue. The sources of inspiration for the base, however, came from farther afield — probably the architectural journals or publications. The use of different types of stone, flamed and polished finishes, pure geometric openings (the requisite square windows and a row of circular portholes) are reminiscent of the work of Michael Graves or even New York designers Kohn, Pedersen, Fox. But the ideas have lost plenty in translation.

Particularly crude are the stylized, oversimplified cornices, sometimes broken, that occur at both the third and seventh floor levels on only the south or de Maisonneuve elevation and on the ninth floor on the east and west elevations. The bull-nosed or triangular form of these cornices

Two distinctive building styles have arisen in recent years: those covered in glass such as the Banque Nationale de Paris . . .

. . . and those clad in stone, such as the Sir Robert Peel condominium block.
Photo by Len Sidaway, The Gazette.

lacks the additional detailing required to perform their original aesthetic, protective, or structural functions. Even the gable-shaped roof lid on the building, intended to enhance its formal directional emphasis toward de Maisonneuve, will likely be an anomaly; the spectacular interior space and climactic views that such dramatic detailing suggest will no doubt be obscured by mechanical equipment.

The decade of the developer's tower has led to a strange denouement — two distinctly different styles of building have developed, one using stone, the other glass. The mirror-glass towers are a little more plentiful, with the Banque Nationale de Paris, the Alliance building at University and Sherbrooke, and the recently completed Maison des Coopérants on the old Christ Church Cathedral grounds being the most visible examples. The best examples in stone are the Industrial Life Tower on McGill College and the IBM-Marathon building on René Lévesque Boulevard.

It is illuminating to look into the origins of these concept buildings. The history of the glass tower can be traced to the German architect Mies van der Rohe and his two projects for glass-enclosed skyscrapers: one in 1919 for Berlin and the other, in 1920, for an imaginary site. His theoretical studies stripped the traditional tower façades of heavy structural materials and superfluous detail, and replaced them with smooth, plain surfaces which were predominantly glass.

These projects represented the crystallization of the idea of making the structure visible. It was Mies van der Rohe's belief that the structural system is the basis of all artistic design and thus must not be hidden by a "chaos of meaningless and trivial forms." His remedy, developed when he designed Chicago's Lake Shore Drive Apartments in 1951, was a curtain-wall system composed of black metal and floor-to-ceiling glass panels. No single architectural idea has had a greater impact on North American cities; it has been repeated and copied for more than 25 years, Montreal's own Westmount Square (for which Mies van der Rohe was the consultant) being a prominent local example.

Since Mies van der Rohe's initial projects, however, the original idea of uncompromising directness of expression has come under a variety of pressures and influences. The transformation of the idea from the drawing board to reality required modifications initiated not by technological advancements but by legal requirements. Recognizing the inability of steel to withstand extreme heat in the event of fire, authorities decreed that all structures be encased in heat-resistant materials.

A dilemma was created for the designer; namely, how to directly express the structure when it was hidden behind the fire-proofing.

The energy crisis gave rise to even more decisive changes. Legislation was passed limiting the amount of transparent glass on a façade to 40 per cent. A design like Westmount Square, with a façade made of approximately 70 per cent glass, is no longer possible. The answer has been to use mirror-glass panels. Whether transparent or opaque, they effectively hide, at least in the daylight, the visual impact of the new legal requirements. Unfortunately they also obscure any reference to structure — like the difference between window and panel — not to mention taking away the fun of watching the hustle and bustle of the human activity within.

Perhaps it could be argued that mirror-glass buildings come closest to the original ideal of the glass tower. Their pristine forms and delightful use of the reflective properties of glass give the impression of an uncompromised idea. However, it has created the situation where possibly the most influential design decision is choosing what type of glass to use — a choice developers in the 1980s have become alarmingly comfortable making.

The problem of the superficiality of this new generation of buildings is even more apparent when one looks at the recently built stone towers. The fashion these days is granite; once again the decision that will have the most important effect on the visual impact of the building is the choice of materials. That proper consideration for other features of design are being sacrificed is a given. Although not as disappointing as Place Canada Trust, the Industrial Life Tower illustrates how the emphasis on the façade can be a little confusing.

Upon initial examination of the façade, our attention is drawn to the building's most distinctive features, the arches at street and penthouse levels. They offer an indication of what the architect had in mind. Clearly he was trying to draw the viewer's attention to the main entrance, which he succeeds in doing. But at what price? From the outside, the arch at the main entrance gives the impression that upon entering the building the viewer will be treated to a grand interior space, somewhat like he might find in Maison Alcan. As anyone who has entered the Industrial Life Tower knows, that is not the case — the main hall is actually only one storey; the rest is rentable office space.

The same type of problem exists at the penthouse level. While the roof arch conjures up ideas of an enclosed winter garden or the ultimate

Place Canada Trust. The trend to designer buildings has resulted in a glass banana with a stone peel.
Courtesy of The Gazette.

IBM has gone to a high-profile New York architectural office to find designers for its new tower on René Lévesque Boulevard.
Courtesy of The Gazette.

in winter discothèques, its real purpose is to hide mechanical equipment. And to top it all off, what appears to be a glass elevator running up the front of the tower — the vertical row of windows that connects the two arches like a giant thermometer — is actually nothing of the sort. Like the rest of the details, they are just part of the façade; they serve no structural purpose whatsoever.

In terms of design, therefore, one can speak about the new generation of buildings without separating them at all. Whether glass or stone, the exterior has almost no influence on the interior: it is purely façade design for the sake of visual impact. In essence, they are the same building; they are just wearing different "skins."

Not all of the new buildings fail so dramatically in their attempt to make a coherent architectural statement. The one true exception to this trend is the IBM-Marathon tower, scheduled to be completed in 1991. IBM, traditionally a pioneer in placing an unusual amount of emphasis on design concerns, have once again seen to it that their tower will have a designer label, that of the New York firm of Kohn, Pederson, Fox. Not since the late 1950s and early 1960s, when internationally renowned consultants such as I.M. Pei, Mies van der Rohe, Pier Luigi Nervi, and partners in the firm of Skidmore, Owens, and Merrill were retained to design some of the city's towers, has such a high-octane team been hired for a project in Montreal.

The presence of such headliners means no simple formula will do. The project will feature a more complicated formal arrangement of office space. The fragmentation of forms, the sculptural treatment of the tower, and, in particular, the configuration at the top of the building — even the radio mast — are reminiscent of the ideas of the Russian Constructivism movement of the 1920s. The effect is that instead of creating an overwhelming visual impact, a subtle balance will be struck. Up close, the fragmentation of the building's huge mass will make it a little less intimidating. Yet from a distance, the tower's distinctive silhouette will make an instantly recognizable feature of the Montreal skyline.

This type of sophisticated thinking appears to be beyond those behind the other projects; their concerns are entirely restricted to surface appearance. In order to properly understand the kind of changes which are been signalled by this emphasis on cosmetics, one merely has to look at how this type of design differs from what might be called the traditional Montreal office tower, such as the Confederation building on Cathcart Street and the Dominion Square building on St. Catherine Street at the corner of Peel.

What sets these two landmarks apart from the new generation of towers is the way they blend into the architecture of the busy street. First of all, instead of being set back, they are built to the sidewalk. Secondly, because they have shops on the ground floor and office space above, they make themselves accessible to the general public. The result is not flashy or even seductive; rather, it is a competent and sometimes elegant solution to a civic problem — how to make private building appear public property.

Taken in this light, the developer's towers suffer by comparison. True, they fulfill the essential desire of any corporation which invests the capital to put up its own tower in a metropolitan area: to show that it is serious about its commitment in the area; and to create a recognizable symbol to heighten its prestige in the eyes of the public. Unfortunately these buildings could be making the statement in any metropolitan area; they make no attempt to conform to the urban landscape of Montreal. In fact, the developer's towers are making Montreal conform to them.

The easiest way to see this essential incongruity is not by looking at the buildings themselves but by looking at what they have done to the street life around them. Behind the Industrial Life Tower, for instance, Mansfield Street, because it has no point of entry, has become little more than a service lane for McGill College Avenue. Stanley Street, which will provide the parking lot entrance for the IBM-Marathon building, will likely suffer the same fate.

Sometimes the street life is able to resist the bullying of a new building. For example, when the Maison des Coopérants complex threatened to eliminate the colourful gathering place of street vendors in front of the cathedral on St. Catherine Street, they simply took their wares across the street. Thank goodness there is still a spot on St. Catherine to rest from mannequins and see some real people.

The problem with the developers' towers is that they are built for boulevards, not for streets, nor, for that matter, people. It is their money, but it also our city. For the first time in my memory developers are, through advertising, marketing their buildings as architectural masterpieces. In self-serving full-page ads in the local press, they are extolling the architectural virtues of their buildings. Carefully crafted prose by advertising copywriters in the guise of architectural critics speak glowingly of "meeting the future with an architectural grace that's the envy of North America."

In reality, we are being presented with conventional, prosaic, commonplace office buildings — nine-foot ceilings, column-free space, state-of-the-art security systems, high-speed elevators — sheathed with smart "graffiti" in stone and glass. Reason, reality, elegance and delight have given way to superficiality and romantic historicism. What it amounts to is a fascination with "skin"; and, at its worst, burlesque.

The age of the developer has brought us shocks which do not endure, architecture reduced to the level of anecdotal statement. Traditional design intentions are being subjected to ridicule; relatively conventional building types are being treated with false grandeur. Burlesque has taken to the streets.

Postmodernism Comes to Montreal

MARK LONDON

Like many social and artistic movements, Postmodernism came late to Montreal. Only in the mid–1980s did the trappings of Postmodern architecture start popping up on the fronts of boutiques in shopping malls, on factories along the Trans-Canada Highway and on downtown office towers.

Proponents welcomed Postmodernism as a movement that would free society from the destruction perpetrated on our cities and culture by the scourge of Modernism. Critics saw it as reactionary and superficial — the phoney and usually clumsy gussying-up of buildings by applying unrelated fragments of architectural nostalgia to their façades. They were both right.

Postmodernism is not a single movement with a clear set of precepts and a consistent look and vision as was Modernism. It is a grab-bag term used to describe anything built since about 1970 that doesn't cling to the maxims of the Modern Movement. Since Postmodernism is the antithesis of Modernism, let us start with a look at this movement as seen through Postmodern eyes.

The Rise of Modernism

Though Montreal's first skyscrapers kept the trappings of traditional design (classical styles executed in stone), builders quickly embraced Modernism during the post-Second World War construction boom. Its

The Royal Bank building on St. Jacques Street is typical of the city's early skyscrapers, built in stone along classical lines.
Photo by Robert Lee, The Gazette.

Postmodernism became mainstream in 1984 when Philip Johnson designed New York's AT&T building, which has been dubbed the Chippendale building.
Courtesy of The Gazette.

stripped-down aesthetic and repetitive forms made for buildings that were quick to erect and cheap to build.

According to the precepts of Modernism, or the International Style, society and its building forms and techniques in the new industrial age were totally different from the past and called for a whole new architecture that was universal and stripped of parochial customs of design. So Modernism rejected the "old-fashioned" manifestations of local traditions, the styles and materials that reflected the history and character of a particular area.

In Modern architecture, forms became simple and abstract. The aim was to purely reflect the building's function, to clearly express its structure, and nothing more. Mies van der Rohe offered the ultimate distillation of Modernism, an elegant, multi-purpose, black box virtually identical wherever in the world it was located and whatever function it housed, from apartments and offices in Westmount Square to a university in Chicago. "Less is more" declared Mies van der Rohe.

The Modern movement also saw industrialization as the solution to the social ills of cities. For example, Le Corbusier showed that by demolishing all the dark, old buildings of Paris (except Notre Dame Cathedral) and replacing them with rows of Place Ville Marie-shaped towers set well apart, much more sunshine could reach the ground where there would be room for broad plazas and wide expressways. Enlightened progress!

The apogee — or last hurrah — of Modernism may well have been right here in Montreal. Expo 67 featured the structural daring-do of Frei Otto's tent (the West German pavilion), Buckminster Fuller's geodesic dome (the American pavilion), and Moishe Safdie's aborted housing experiment with industrialization at Habitat 67. But despite its high-minded ideals, Modernism began to fall from this heady success into disfavour.

The Decline of Modernism

In the 1960s and 1970s, Modernism was increasingly associated with everything that was wrong with the post-war city — the destruction of neighbourhoods, the uprooting of families and the demolition of historic buildings. Change was taking place at a dizzying pace and on a massive scale. It seemed that everything familiar and comfortable in people's surroundings was being systematically eradicated, only to be replaced with gigantic, impersonal shoe boxes designed in the Modern style. A single building, with one function, designed by one person and built in a year or two might cover a whole block, and replace dozens of older buildings erected over time with their rich variety of materials, designs and uses. The new buildings were tall but were more likely to be jammed together cheek by jowl than be separated by Le Corbusier's broad sunny areas.

In fact, the areas between the buildings were falling into rapid decline. The "me-generation" was spending an increasing proportion of money on the private realm (individual homes and offices) rather than the collective realm (high-quality building exteriors, well-designed and maintained streets, parks, and public buildings). A Modern house might have the most luxurious sauna and sunken whirlpool bath behind the simplest, starkest Modern façade; on Wall Street, only a few feet separated the fabulously appointed boardrooms in the Modern head offices of the world's most powerful corporations from the deteriorating squalor of the subway.

People became upset. Concern about Modernism was not so much a question of architectural style but of how our cities were being developed. Postmodernism emerged out of a desire that they be more human in scale and relate better to our cultural traditions.

The Rise of Postmodernism

The rejection of Modernism and the birth of Postmodernism in city planning and architecture can be traced to the publication of two books. Jane Jacobs' *The Death and Life of Great American Cities* in 1961 argued that the abstract ideas and the radical change advocated by Modern planners were destroying rather than helping our cities. Robert Venturi, in *Complexity and Contradiction in Architecture*, published in 1967, set out the philosophical basis for Postmodernism. "Less is a bore" he quipped.

Another father of Postmodernism — though unheralded — was Walt Disney. The commercial success of his Magic Kingdoms demonstrated how much people loved environments that were diametric opposites of the Modern ideal. The anti-Modernist sentiment was also strong in the increasingly powerful heritage movement (ironically the same movement now working to preserve the best Modernist structures).

One of the first Postmodernist architects to come to Montreal preaching the gospel of the new movement was Robert Stern. In an Alcan architectural lecture in 1976, he blasted Modernism for destroying all that people held dear in their built environment only to replace it with abstract and inhuman manifestations of the machine age. He showed slides of recent suburban housing (the type dismissed by the architectural profession as commercial pandering to the basest common taste) and he asserted that these tract builders were the true noble craftsmen of the age because they simply continued to build good, solid homes in traditional local styles that people liked. They built Cape Cod houses in Cape Cod and Colonial style houses in the former colonies (although admittedly they sometimes got the two mixed up)

Postmodernists argued that there is nothing wrong with building a house today that looks just like one erected a century ago. People still want living rooms, dining rooms, kitchens and bedrooms; homes are still generally built of brick, wood, glass and plaster. True, bathrooms and kitchens have evolved, but surprisingly, the revolutionary technology that was supposed to transform the House of Tomorrow into a modern, slick, high-tech "machine for living" ended up by being subtly incorporated into our traditional homes. The TV is not room-sized but is discreetly tucked away on a shelf or behind wood-panelled doors; the device that lets us calculate like a whiz and communicate with the world does not require a NASA control room in every home; it is a lap-top computer that fits nicely into the antique roll-top desk in the den.

Two basic tenets of Postmodernism are urbanism and historicism. Urbanism involves the effort to make a new building fit into its context rather than Modernism's approach of contrasting with, or often, simply ignoring its surroundings. This is usually done through an understanding and respect for the urban patterns in the area, ranging from the way people move to the form and materials of neighbouring buildings and, in some cases, even a matching of the design details of older neighbours.

Historicism is the use of traditional historical styles or designs. Postmodernists repudiated the notion that architecture must reject the past to meet the needs of the future. They questioned the relatively recent notion that originality was necessarily an important objective in architecture. In the past, they argued, architects and artists forthrightly copied from the masters, seeking to refine and perfect rather than change just for the sake of being different.

In many cases, historicism merely became the superficial appliqué of decorative details from the past, an odd pediment or a stylized, oversized column. These were distorted caricatures of historical styles, showing a token reference to history but refusing to embrace the philosophy of traditional design. This lead to what was called "Xerox architecture" where architects would just copy bits and pieces of old building designs and collage them onto the façades of their buildings. Perhaps the architects, trained in the Modernist period and never having learned the design principles of traditional architecture, used the Postmodernist label to excuse their poorly thought out designs.

Postmodernism became mainstream in 1984 when it was embraced by one of the most significant Modernists: Philip Johnson. His design for the world headquarters of the AT&T building in New York was dubbed the Chippendale building because the cut-out at the top looked like it came from an antique piece of furniture. Even before it was completed, it spawned knock-offs around the world.

Montreal's Industrial Life Tower is one. It and Maison Alcan are two of the earliest Postmodernist buildings in Montreal and they illustrate well two different approaches to this architectural movement: the first is a Modern building disguised in Postmodern clothes while the second looks Modern but in design philosophy is really a more fundamental embracing of Postmodernist ideals.

At the Industrial Life Tower, Postmodernism is only skin deep. True, granite walls give it a greater sense of solidity than earlier office towers and the shapes along the roof line differentiate it from the standard box. However, in its basic conception, this is just another Modern high-rise office tower — a huge shaft set well back from the street behind a concrete plaza. It does not fit into a traditional urban form much better than any of the other similar towers on René Lévesque or de Maisonneuve Boulevards.

In contrast, Maison Alcan, with its slick, high-tech aluminum façade, might at first glance be seen as a purely Modern building. However it is clear that the architects' main aim was to fit the building into its traditional, low-scale context, not to stand out as a highly visible, free-standing object. Also, its design follows certain traditional principles of building organization: its odd shape comes from an effort to integrate into its urban context rather than to create a building as an

The distinctive shape and granite facing mark
Place Montreal Trust as a Postmodern building.
Photo by Bryan Demchinsky.

In the Industrial Life Tower, Postmodernism is only skin deep — it is basically a Modern high-rise with a few added touches such as the shape of the roof line.
Photo by Robert Lee, The Gazette.

isolated object; its ground floor houses lively restaurants and shops as opposed to the institutional uses of Industrial Life's ground floor.

A Postmodern Field Guide

For those prowling the streets of Montreal in search of Postmodernist buildings, here is a field guide of the more obvious characteristics that tend to distinguish them from their Modern predecessors.

At the bottom, much more emphasis is given to the design of the first four metres of the façade, the part most perceived by passersby. The prime consideration in determining the position of walls is how best to enclose the street or space outside the building rather than simply housing the interior requirements, For example, in a densely built urban environment, the Postmodern building is likely to hug the sidewalk instead of being set back on an ill-defined and unused plaza. Compare, for example, the 1988 Place Montréal Trust building on McGill College Avenue with Place Ville Marie. Also on a commercial street, its ground floor probably has shops accessible from the sidewalk instead of merely a blank wall.

At the top, the flat roofline is no longer de rigeur. In Montreal, cornices, false mansards, peaks and pediments abound. Office towers have tops that harken back to early, pre-war skyscrapers. Compare Maison des Coopérants' owl-ears top with the flat top of, say, the Canadian Imperial Bank of Commerce skyscraper at the corner of René Lévesque and Peel Street.

The Postmodern building is built of, or at least faced with, solid materials: its walls look like they are strong enough to hold up the roof. In general, masonry is back in, as are the local materials that gave each city its special character. In Montreal, red brick and greystone are reappearing in place of Modernism's all-glass curtain walls and its extensive use of metal and concrete.

Since the walls are made of solid materials, the windows are clearly defined. This gives the Postmodern building a sense of scale often lacking in Modern structures. You can actually see how many storeys a building has. In general, the location, sizes and shapes of door and window openings tend to be more varied in a Postmodern building; windows are more likely to be vertical rectangles than horizontal strips. Compare the Industrial Life Tower to the Banque Nationale de Paris

Maison Alcan, which integrates old buildings with a new office tower — connected by the Atrium seen here — is much closer to the spirit of Postmodernism.
Photo by Len Sidaway, The Gazette.

facing it across McGill College Avenue. The interiors are likely to be made up of well-defined rooms instead of the continuous, free-flowing space of Modern structures.

Another feature that sets Postmodernist buildings apart is their use of complexity and contradiction. With both Classical styles and the Modern Movement, there were clear sets of rules and each work was resolved as a complete and consistent entity. With Postmodernism there is often a somewhat uncomfortable juxtaposition of several styles and forms.

When it comes to design details, however, there is a great diversity in approach by Postmodern architects. Some use modern details, others use stylized caricatures of traditional designs, while still others base their details directly on historical styles. Recently, there has been increasing interest in a return to classicism, and at least one architect, Britain's Quinlan Terry, designs buildings that are indistinguishable from those built centuries ago.

What's Next?

With any style — whether a genre of music or a school of furniture design — the most sensitive and skillful practitioners produce great works of art, the competent journeyman produce good workaday products for daily needs, and the talentless incompetents produce pretentious drivel that gives the style a bad name. This is true of both Modernism and Postmodernist architecture. With Postmodernism, some of the worst examples are the downtown towers and suburban office buildings, which scatter a variety of arches and pediments using traditional forms without any understanding of the specific roles these are supposed to play in architecture.

In contrast, some of the best examples of Postmodernism are infill apartment buildings in the McGill Ghetto and in Plateau Mount Royal, simple brick buildings with shops on the ground floor that fit into and add considerably to the quality of the streets.

For the past few decades, architecture seems to have been caught in a frenzy of styles where the right look changes as quickly as the dresses from Yves St. Laurent or the songs on the Top 40. This frenzy was nurtured by the architectural magazines which, by their nature, are always seeking dramatic new visual images, however superficial they may be.

After the radical swing of the pendulum from Modernism to Postmodernism, current thought seems to be evolving in the direction of an architecture that is not so much a radical opposition to Modernism but rather an evolution of Modernism, combining the best of both periods into a coherent vocabulary.

The Canadian Centre for Architecture is a good example. It was designed using a well thought-out, consistent design philosophy that could be labelled Postmodern Classicism. Its approach to overall form and organization and its choice of materials is clearly inspired by the past and its surroundings, but the details are nothing ever found in the 19th century.

Postmodernism has helped bring the emphasis in architecture from steel and engineering to people, urbanism and history. However, today the term is so associated with the superficial hodge-podge approach that it is largely discredited and will probably fade away. If a coherent philosophy of building emerges that is more responsive to people's needs than either Modernism or Postmodernism, someone will have to make up a new name for it.

HERITAGE

The demolition of the Van Horne mansion on Sherbrooke Street in 1973 set off a reaction whose effects are still felt in Montreal. Out of that act of destruction was born the movement that continues to serve as the guardian of the city's architectural heritage.

Since the 1970s, the value of heritage buildings has gained currency. Developers and city officials must now think twice before attempting to erase a building of any historical significance. More often today, an older building will be recycled, renovated, or at least some parts of it will be saved.

However, defenders of heritage buildings cannot rest easy. For all the change in attitude, buildings continue to be lost — the Queen's Hotel is only the most blatant example. Preservation means more than simply saving old buildings — other aspects of the urban landscape are equally precious. And much of the new wave of preservation is of dubious merit. Is saving bits and pieces of buildings the right approach? Issues such as these keep the heritage debate alive.

Architectural Heritage: More Than Preserving Old Buildings

JOSHUA WOLFE

For many years, the concept of heritage was simply a reverence for buildings connected to an incident or hero of history — caricaturized as the "George Washington slept here" approach to architectural evaluation. Only a building closely linked to an important figure was judged worth saving. More recently, the idea of what constitutes heritage has broadened.

A Montreal example of a building of clearly historical importance is Château Ramezay. This manor house was inhabited originally by the French governor of Montreal, Claude de Ramezay, and later, in the 1770s, by Benjamin Franklin and generals Richard Montgomery and Benedict Arnold, who were part of an American occupation force. It was also the seat of government during the mid-1800s.

Its venerable age and its links to important figures and events in history make Château Ramezay a classic example of a historic building. In fact, it was the first building classified as a historic monument by the provincial government, back in 1929.

Another example of a building associated with the life or activities of an important person and with an important event in history, is the house at 1395 Overdale Avenue, which was once the residence of Louis-Hippolyte Lafontaine at the time when he was prime minister of what was then called the Province of Canada (comprising Ontario and Quebec).

The Lafontaine house was also the site of an important moment in Canadian history, when Tory rioters pursued Lafontaine to his house after setting fire to the parliament buildings in Place d'Youville.

Although it is probably untrue that bullet holes still mark the façade of the house on Overdale, the structure is still worth preserving: the parliament building was destroyed during the 1849 riot and the house is the only physical reminder of that step in Canada's evolution to democracy. In 1988 the house was embroiled in a new controversy when tenants on Overdale were evicted to make way for a massive condominium project. The house was spared demolition (the fate of other buildings at the site) and now stands empty with the condo scheme on hold.

Since the 1960s, North Americans have come to realize that there are a number of different criteria to determine whether a building should be preserved. In addition to historic events, esthetics are also used to judge which buildings are worth saving. For example, some of the houses on Laval Avenue near St. Louis Square are fine examples of 19th-century design: their attractive dormer windows have been used in countless tourist brochures to illustrate the wonders of Montreal's traditional architecture.

Of course, aesthetic judgment is somewhat less straightforward than the identification of important events in history. For many years, most 19th-century architecture was condemned by Modernists offended by what they considered excessive ornamentation. They denounced it as a hodge-podge of styles from across the centuries that were only dimly understood. It was only in the 1970s that Montrealers began to appreciate the craftsmanship, creativity and eclecticism of the city's early building styles.

Now it is Modernist buildings that are threatened. Recent renovations of Place Ville Marie and Westmount Square have been condemned for violating the aesthetic principles of an important period in 20th-century architecture. While some preservationists may appreciate traditional architecture more than the austere "less is more" of the Modernists, they still want to see the best examples of each architectural movement preserved.

A third type of heritage is the one that is perhaps hardest justify to the layman. It has to do with building techniques — architectonics and engineering.

Grain Elevator No. 2, at the foot of Place Jacques Cartier, acquired international fame when the Swiss architect Le Corbusier included a photograph of it in his seminal work *Vers une Architecture*. He was struck by the bold massiveness of this concrete structure and considered it a

The Château de Ramezay on Notre Dame Street
exemplifies the traditional notion of heritage —
preserving an old building that has historical associations.
Photo by Len Sidaway, The Gazette.

Another facet of heritage is the ensemble — groups of
buildings that together create historical or other associations.
The houses on Henri-Julien Avenue near St. Jean Baptiste
church on Rachel Street are a good example of the ensemble.
Photo by Robert Lee, The Gazette.

Houses of Laval Avenue are worth preserving
because of their aesthetic as well as historic merit.
Photo by Robert Lee, The Gazette.

Aside from buildings, popular public spaces
such as St. Louis Square deserve protection.
Photo by Richard Arless Jr., The Gazette.

prototypical example of beauty derived from a purely functional structure. Another example is the Lachine Canal, whose intricate system of locks make it an engineering feat.

The difficulty with architectonic value is that it may have nothing to do with aesthetic appeal. But since architecture is a marriage of art and technology, its heritage must include both elements. Grain Elevator No. 2 was demolished not only because some considered it ugly, but also because it was out of scale with Place Jacques Cartier and blocked the view of the St. Lawrence River. For this reason, Montreal preservationists were divided as to whether it should be demolished, depending on whether they considered urban design or architectural preservation more important.

A fourth criterion for preservation is the ensemble. The International Council of Monuments and Sites (a non-governmental organization associated with UNESCO) has established that heritage includes not only individual buildings of high intrinsic value, but also groupings of less important structures that form a coherent set. In such a situation, the whole is greater than the sum of its parts.

A group of buildings creates an unmistakable setting. Thus, it is not just an individual historic monument, such as St. Jean Baptiste Church (Rachel Street East, designed by Casimir Saint-Jean in 1912) that merits preservation, but also the hundreds of modest homes that line nearby streets such as Henri-Julien and Drolet. These were the homes of parishioners of St. Jean Baptiste. They should be saved not only because of their intrinsic value (which is of secondary importance in comparison to that of the church) but also because of what they represent historically. Removed from their context, deprived of other buildings of the same period, individual monuments such as churches are merely mute vestiges of our collective past. Preserving the neighbourhood of the people who contributed to the construction of this majestic church tells us much about their values and priorities.

Religious and institutional complexes such as the Mother House of the Grey Nuns on René Lévesque Boulevard or McGill University also form ensembles of undeniable quality.

Another form of heritage encompasses unbuilt parts of the urban environment. It includes parks, playgrounds and other public spaces that are integral to the city's landscape. The controversy that erupted in 1989 when the city proposed building a parking lot under St. Louis Square (an idea that was quickly shelved after area residents protested) is an indication of the importance of these places to the public.

Disregard for this form of heritage can have consequences as devastating to the city as any number of demolitions. One has only recall that Champ de Mars, today a parking lot, was once the city's finest park. Meanwhile, the concrete makeover of nearby Viger Square serves as a reminder that poorly conceived refurbishment of public spaces can also produce unfortunate results.

Finally, archeological ruins also merit preservation because they can teach us a great deal about the past — how people lived, the kind of work they did, how the city evolved. While bits and pieces of Montreal's history will be showcased in archeological exhibits during celebrations in 1992 marking the 350th anniversary of the founding of Montreal, the largest remaining piece of the fortifications that once surrounded the old city was eliminated during the excavation of the parking garage that is part of the Chaussegros de Léry project, just east of city hall. Ironically, the Chaussegros de Léry development, a residential project which is to open in 1992, is named in honour of the French colonial-era engineer who designed the city's fortifications.

Few buildings or sites in Montreal have any official heritage status. While the criteria listed above are accepted by governmental agencies throughout the world, heritage in Quebec is not given as broad a definition. Until recently, only the provincial Ministry of Cultural Affairs could officially certify the heritage value of a structure through its powers to "classify" buildings and create historic districts. Renovation and demolition of such buildings is not permitted without the permission of the ministry.

In addition to protecting buildings in this way, the ministry has created the "macro-inventaire" in order to identify all buildings of primary and secondary architectural importance in Quebec. While it is supposed to be a comprehensive listing, the macro-inventaire has some curious omissions.

An example is the Grosvenor Apartment building, an English Renaissance-style structure that forms a pleasing corner piece at Sherbrooke and Guy Streets. Its architects, Findley and Spence, were responsible for the design of a number of impressive commercial and religious buildings in Montreal. The English Renaissance-style apartment building is a delightful part of Sherbrooke Street.

The Church of Saint Andrew and Saint Paul (Redpath Avenue, at the corner of Sherbrooke) is also excluded, probably because it was built

Grain Elevator No. 2 (now demolished) looking southwest, Port of Montreal. Grain elevators have an architectonic value, representing design and engineering achievements of the past.
Photo by David Miller © copyright.

in 1932, later than the macro-inventaire's arbitrary cut-off date of 1930.

The date of construction is not very useful for evaluating heritage. Once a 50-year delay between construction and recognition was the norm. However, with the shortening of the lifespan of buildings — afflicted as we are with what social critic Christopher Lash has called the "narcissism of the present" — even 25-year-old buildings are not immune to dismissal as passé.

In contrast, New York City has given heritage landmark status to Lever House, barely 30 years old. The second McDonald's restaurant, of the same vintage, has also been accorded this honour because it is a prototype that influenced a great many buildings in North America.

It is important to permit gradations in the evaluation of heritage architecture. One way to fine-tune the process is to create different categories of buildings, identifying them in terms of national, regional and local importance.

An example of a building of national importance is the Cormier house at 1418 Pine Avenue West. Ernest Cormier, the architect of the Université de Montréal, participated in building the United Nations headquarters in New York City. His home is an arresting exposition of Art Deco, one of the most important examples of that style in Canada. In addition to the designing the structure, he was responsible for its interior and furnishings.

The "west end" branch of the Bank of Montreal (now Guardian Trust branch at Mansfield and St. Catherine Streets) would be considered of regional importance. Built in 1889, it was the first branch office of a bank in the city.

A building such as Cherrier School, on Cherrier Street near St. Hubert Street, is of local interest and is an integral part of its neighbourhood.

An alternative classification would be to identify buildings of primary value, those that form architectural groupings, and those that merely contribute to their surroundings because their appearance is generally complementary with more important buildings. In using either type of hierarchy, the higher the category, the more stringently would controls be applied.

Heritage conservation has evolved to include many different types of buildings and spaces with many different historical, architectural and social elements. While this does not mean that buildings must never be demolished, the onus should be on the individual proposing to eliminate the structure to explain why the new construction is superior to what is threatened.

Montreal still has enough open space along suburban thoroughfares and on downtown parking lots to permit us to preserve much of the old while still allowing for new construction.

The Three Rs: Restoration, Renovation and Recycling

SUSAN BRONSON

One of the most notable changes in Montreal's recent architecture is that preservation of buildings has become not only popular but prestigious. Demolition, once the easy way of coping with vestiges of the past, is now generally condemned, while the "3 Rs" — restoration, renovation and recycling — offer culturally responsible, socially acceptable and even economically viable alternatives to new construction.

This essay will discuss these three approaches to preservation and their application to Montreal architecture of the past decade.

Commendable architecture no longer implies the mere rescue of a landmark and honourable intentions for its future. Today, a good solution to an architectural problem involving an existing building presents a far greater challenge than starting from scratch.

Successful preservation depends on a strong idea and a realistic vision. This must be shared not only by the owner, who generates and finances the project, and the architect, who is responsible for its design and realization, but also by the various government officials, who generally have the final say in its approval and sometimes even contribute to its financing.

The attribute that distinguishes exemplary preservation is quality. This applies to design and construction on three basic levels: theory (the development of an attitude towards the relationship between old and new, in terms of both general approach and particular details); technology (the resolution of complex and often unforeseen conservation and construction problems not encountered in new construction); and practice (the respectful integration of contemporary requirements).

After all the thoughtless demolitions and ruthless retrofits of the 1960s and 1970s, it is refreshing to see a renewed interest in Montreal's incredibly rich architectural heritage. Promising ideas and workable visions about what to do with existing buildings have not been lacking in the 1980s. However, the full potential of these inspirations is often compromised by lack of expertise and experience, not to mention standards and guidelines, in the theoretical, technical and practical aspects of their implementation.

Each of the 3 Rs has its own mandate, challenges and implications. Faced with an existing building, the choice of the appropriate type of intervention, or combination of interventions, is the first and most critical decision. It depends on many factors related to both the building itself — its architectural value, its historical associations, its condition, its location, the zoning and code restrictions to which it must comply — and the priorities of the day — social expectations, cultural preoccupations and, of course, marketability.

Restoration

Restoration implies the return of a building, or part of one, to a previous state in its history. A building that merits such attention is either already a landmark, or has the architectural and/or historical potential for being one. It is restored either to its original state, when it was closest in spirit to its design conception, or to a significant period in its evolution.

In either case, it is probable that layers of interventions work will have to be carefully removed to uncover previous architectural finishes and features, should they still exist. For this reason, most restoration work requires extensive knowledge of historical styles, materials and methods, as well as traditional and contemporary ways of replicating them.

In addition, authentic restoration projects entail considerable research into the history of the building. Often, its evolution and clues for its restoration are revealed only through careful study, exploratory demolition and laboratory testing of remaining details, supplemented by whatever drawings, photographs and written accounts may be available.

Though often belittled as uncreative or imitative, it happens that restoration demands more expertise, and inevitably more research, time and money, than renovation or recycling. Usually a non-lucrative venture, its rewards can be rated in terms of their effect on the image, rather than the pocketbook, of the sponsor. In Canada, most restoration projects are largely government funded, and their timing often corresponds to upcoming elections or anniversaries.

One of the most extensive restoration projects in the city's history was the rejuvenation of more than 100 churches in the Montreal area (1983–1985). Co-ordinated by the Comité de construction et d'Art sacré de l'Archevêché (founded in 1976), the program was sponsored by the federal and provincial governments as a job-creation scheme. It reflects the reassuring if belated realization that religious buildings constitute an irreplaceable part of Montreal's architectural and cultural heritage.

Ten years earlier, the very existence of many of the churches that benefited from this program — such as J.O. Marchand's boat-shaped Ste. Cunégonde of 1906 on St. Jacques Street and Victor Bourgeau's Gothic-inspired St. Joseph de Montréal of 1862 on Richmond Street — was severely threatened as their surrounding neighbourhoods were ruthlessly razed. Furthermore, new attitudes imposed by the Vatican II Council of 1964 — whose mandate was to update and simplify not only the Roman Catholic liturgy but its places of worship — led to the radical transformation of some of the finest architectural interiors in the city.

The restorations included some renovation: long overdue maintenance and upkeep (roof, window and masonry repairs), updating and renewal (construction of ramps for the handicapped and installation of new heating and lighting systems), the reconstruction of original architectural features (replacement of statuary, altars and communion rails removed in the 1960s) and the replenishment of finishes (re-creation of original colour schemes and gold leaf highlights).

The restoration of the interior of l'Eglise de la Visitation at Sault au Récollet, the oldest church on the Island of Montreal, deserves special mention. Built over a period of a century (1749–1850), it represents the work of some of Quebec's most renowned artisans and architects. In 1984 and 1985, its rich and irreplaceable late 17th and early 18th-century interior decoration was returned to its original splendour. The Quebec sculptor Roger Dallaire spent two years restoring the church's sculptural motifs, including the gold-leaf decorations on the splendid wood-vaulted ceiling crafted by Fleury David between 1816 and 1830. This restoration resulted in the re-creation of a sensational interior space and revived forms of craftsmanship that had been given up for lost.

The Maison George-Etienne Cartier represents a different kind of restoration program. Carried out under the supervision of Parks Canada between 1973 and 1985, this project required exploratory demolition, exhaustive research and even public consultation. The pair of semi-detached townhouses which once belonged to Cartier is located at the corner of Notre Dame and Berri Streets. After considerable study, it was decided that the east house should be recycled into an interpretation centre honouring this important Canadian political figure, and that the west building should be restored as a "museum-house" decorated to represent a bourgeois Montreal home during the period of his tenancy (1862–71).

Though not authentic in the sense of a totally accurate and faithful reconstruction, the restoration of the east house aimed at re-creating the spirit of the Victorian era. Theatrical devices, such as stage-setting, tape-recorded conversations and simulated lighting, were introduced to make the restored rooms more convincing and understandable to visitors of all ages.

Perhaps the greatest challenge of restoration work is the respectful integration of contemporary requirements that allow public enjoyment of these landmark buildings. In the case of Eglise de la Visitation, lighting and sprinkler heads have been added; in the Maison George-Etienne Cartier, guard rails and exit signs were required. The insensitive design or incorporation of such features can destroy the impact of an otherwise impressive restoration project.

Renovation

Unlike restoration, renovation has no obligation to duplicate the past. Rather, it frankly acknowledges the realities of the present and updates any elements of a building's architecture that do not meet the requirements of its contemporary counterparts.

The mandate of this type of rehabilitation is almost always based on marketability. Its mission is to please but its ultimate motive is to make money. Depending on the clientele and the budget available, the work can vary in scope from the simple cosmetic treatment of the existing surfaces of a building to the drastic destruction and replacement of its architectural features.

Not surprisingly, the building types most affected by this exercise in marketing are those that correspond to the new construction of the day.

In Montreal, the proliferation of world-class hotels, shiny office towers and light-filled shopping malls woke up the owners of the comparatively dowdy old buildings and made them realize that they had better spruce up or sell out.

Hotels, for instance, are prime targets for cosmetic renovations. Over the past few decades, Montreal lost a number of favourite retreats: the Laurentian and the Queen's fell to the wrecker's ball, while the Mount Royal Hotel and the remaining wing of the Windsor Hotel were recycled into more marketable enterprises.

As new facilities started to attract a larger portion of the city's visitors, the owners of the Bonaventure and Château Champlain, so modern when they were built for Expo 67 two decades earlier, the Queen Elizabeth, a 30-year-old structure, and even the Ritz-Carlton, with its status as the only remaining luxury hotel built before 1950, realized that their star ratings depended on the renovation of their interiors.

So, at considerable expense to their operations, these hotels embarked on ambitious facelifts. By 1990, they too will be able to claim all the modern conveniences of most contemporary hotels: tasteful artwork, indirect lighting, patterned carpets, designer colours, Postmodern touches and marble tile bathrooms. In addition, they will boast that extra bonus acquired only with age: the newly popular and prestigious "charm of yesteryear."

Similar tactics have been used in the retail sector. Even before the glittering new Place Montréal Trust opened, downtown shopping centre owners were catching on to the fact that consumers of the 1980s are attracted to new kinds of shopping mall motifs: shiny surfaces, light-filled atriums with tropical plants and, most important, classy fast-food markets, where one can sip a cappuccino and watch people go by, or gobble down a Mexican meal while on the run between the hectic obligations of contemporary living.

The exquisitely designed underground shopping promenades of such Modern monuments as I.M. Pei's Place Ville Marie of 1959 and Mies van der Rohe's Westmount Square of 1966 — so novel and imposing in their glory days — suddenly seemed dark and dated. In addition, their interiors showed the inevitable signs of wear and tear, and their exteriors suffered from the severity of Montreal's climate.

The owners of these Modern monuments — being businessmen and realists — must have considered that the pure restoration of architectural features would neither regain declining business assets nor attract tenants

Maison Alcan has proved to be one of the most successful examples of recycling, preserving the Berkeley Hotel and several greystones on Sherbrooke Street.
Photo by Gordon Beck, The Gazette.

Renovation of Mies van der Rohe's Westmount Square has provoked debate about how much tampering with the original architecture should be allowed during the refurbishment of Modern landmarks.
Photo by Len Sidaway, The Gazette.

who had been lured to their more glamorous competitors. Not only did deteriorating materials have to be replaced; contemporary marketing expectations had to be met.

The renovation of Place Ville Marie's shopping corridors (1987–88) included adding gently arched ceilings with indirect lighting, the introduction of marble tile floors and the replacement of the once elegant bistro-type bar in the middle with a fast-food centre. The sunken courtyards formerly used as summertime terrace cafés were covered by projecting skylights to provide year-round sun-filled accommodation for the new generation of fast-food eaters. Outside, on the mall above, the pyramidal skylights, surrounded by plots of grass and variously articulated modular spaces, have completely transformed the nature of the once wide open plaza.

Place Ville Marie has once again become a popular, though less exclusive, people place. But this first major transformation of one of Montreal's most eloquent expressions of the International Style has raised an important question: Have we arrived at the point when a Modern monument constitutes "heritage" and, if so, does an intervention of this nature not betray the original architectural integrity of our most recent past?

This issue came to a head in 1989 when a renovation scheme at Westmount Square sparked heated reactions among Montreal's fans of Mies van der Rohe and Modernism. The proposed projecting skylights and glass entranceways were compared to warts on the originally open mall; the replacement of the plaza's weather-worn travertine paving stones (not entirely appropriate to Montreal's severe climate) with granite ones and the discontinuity this introduced between the exterior mall and the interior lobbies (where the travertine was still in acceptable condition) was condemned as desecration.

An angry protest resulted in the owner's decision to put a hold on the work, which was well underway. At the time of writing, the design of the proposed modifications is being carefully reconsidered before construction resumes.

This turn of events is significant. The comparison of the proposed renovation of Westmount Square to "changing the harmonies of Beethoven's Fifth Symphony," as one critic suggested, indicates that, for the first time in Montreal's history, Modernist monuments are perhaps more worthy of respectful restoration than fashionable renovation. From this debate, a new challenge presents itself to architects: can a restored monument respond to contemporary marketing expectations? Can its "heritage significance" be the feature that distinguishes it from its newer counterparts and make it marketable?

Recycling

Recycling, often referred to as "adaptive re-use" or "revitalization," is the practice of rehabilitating buildings to suit purposes other than those for which they were originally intended. It goes back to ancient times and presents a convenient and economical alternative to demolition and new construction.

An empty building, subject to deterioration and a target of vandalism, constitutes a potential danger to its neighbourhood. For the past two decades, the answer to this threat has most often been to demolish the building and replace it with either a parking lot or a high-rise. Recently, recycling has become an acceptable alternative to this trend.

Revitalization acknowledges the dynamic spirit of buildings — the qualities that allow them to evolve and accommodate vastly different functions. An added factor is the cost of new construction. Adapting a building to a new use has also become economically viable.

The best candidates for recycling are those buildings that have outlived the use for which they were designed, but are structurally sound and architecturally interesting. They range from architectural landmarks to modest structures of a distinct building type.

Montreal has always had plenty of recyclable buildings in both categories. All over the city, countless warehouses, schools, hotels, movie houses, garages and religious buildings have stood empty or under-used with the constant threat of the wrecker's ball hanging over them. In the 1980s, many of these buildings were adapted to functions totally unrelated to their original uses.

Maison Alcan (1983) led the way by recycling a series of late 19th-century greystones and the early 20th-century Berkeley Hotel into offices. The project also included the restoration of the exteriors and selected portions of the interiors of these Sherbrooke Street buildings, as well as their connection to a new low-rise aluminum-clad office building by a handsome atrium. This skylit space, which allows daylight

Maison George-Etienne Cartier was restored
and turned into a museum by Parks Canada.
Photo by Bryan Demchinsky.

Recycling has turned an old auto showroom on St. Catherine Street into one of the city's most successful shopping malls — Le Faubourg.
Photo by Len Sidaway, The Gazette.

to enter both the old and new buildings, doubles as an interior public square where exhibits and concerts are enjoyed by Alcan employees and the public. The complex not only became the most prestigious corporate headquarters in the city, but served as an important precedent by demonstrating the potential of a successful integration of old and new.

The owners of two former hotels on Peel Street were quick to follow Maison Alcan's lead. Le Windsor (1987), which now houses the offices of some of Montreal's top firms, exploits the historical associations attached to the once grand hotel. A soaring atrium provides the offices in the remaining wing of the old Windsor Hotel with daylight and allows one privileged tenant the bonus of a light-filled interior courtyard. In addition, the recycled building boasts unique features that its contemporary counterparts cannot offer: its restored exterior and renovated entrance lobby, grand hall and ballrooms give the building the hint of past glory, a most marketable feature.

Up the street, Les Cours Mont-Royal (1987) took the hotel re-use concept one step further by introducing into the heart of downtown, a mixed-use complex that includes luxury condominiums, prestigious office space, Yuppie-targeted stores, an Egyptian-styled cinema and a high-class fast-food emporium. The various facilities are grouped around a series of skylit courtyards. Like Le Windsor, this project offers its own unique features: remnants of the former grandeur of this once elegant hotel are reflected by its decorated ceilings, the grand central staircase, and the restoration of the renowned Kon-Tiki bar.

New life was brought to St. Catherine Street West when Le Faubourg (1987), was created from a modest but handsome brick building designed as a garage and auto showroom. It was converted into a market hall based on Boston's Faneuil Market. Montrealers watched with trepidation as the entire structure was precariously supported to allow the addition of lower floors required for parking and cinemas. The levels just below and just above the street, housing specialty shops and every kind of fast-food outlet imaginable, are sprinkled with fountains, plants and terraces with tables offering unlimited people-watching opportunities.

East on St. Catherine Street, Métropolis (1987) exploited the architectural qualities of the splendid interior of the old Théâtre Empire by integrating its remaining decorative elements into a spectacular performance hall and night club.

Perhaps the greatest challenge of recycling lies in the ability to select new uses compatible with the buildings that will house them, and to selectively exploit the existing architectural qualities so that they distinguish the project from its contemporary counterparts.

All the noteworthy projects have been discussed here only in terms of their intentions and ideas. On this level, they are successful examples of preservation. They enhance their neighbourhoods, offer popular and prestigious alternatives to new construction and allow the public an opportunity to enjoy aspects of the city's heritage that would otherwise have been lost or forgotten.

However, in terms of the quality of their design and realization, all of these projects could stand improvement. Most Montreal preservation projects of the 1980s have yet to master that precarious relationship between old and new — the sensitive and consistent handling of details where the two come together, the selective incorporation of new materials and methods with old ones, the respectful integration of contemporary requirements such as exit signs and access for the handicapped.

These shortcomings, by no means unique to Montreal, are largely the result of a general lack of expertise and experience in the field of preservation. This is shared by owners, architects and government officials alike: owners still sometimes impose overly restrictive budget constraints; architects continue to lack the expertise required for certain theoretical, technical or practical preservation decisions; government officials continue to allow the demolition of potentially reusable buildings (Cormier's seaplane hangar, Grain Elevator No. 1 and the Queen's Hotel, to name a few, were lost during the 1980s), and sometimes their input tends to restrict, rather than improve, the possibility of a successful preservation effort.

On one hand, the growing popularity and prestige of preservation has had a positive impact. The increasing familiarity of its particular problems has led to more ready solutions. Standards and guidelines are being set, technical literature is becoming increasingly available, specialized courses are being offered and, most importantly, we now have an expanding repertoire of case studies to learn from.

At the same time, the marketing potential of this approach to architecture is being exploited in a way that is not particularly commendable. The practice of tacking an insensitive new structure on to an existing building or its remains has become a money-making venture disguised as preservation. Today, even new construction, such as the Sir Robert

Peel condominium tower, is being marketed on the basis of its nostalgic association with "a bygone era."

If the architecture of the 1980s is characterized by the recognition of the potential of preservation, then the goal of the 1990s should be respectful interventions that reflect the quality that Montreal's irreplaceable architecture of the past deserves.

The Façade Fad: Saving Face Isn't Always Enough

JOSHUA WOLFE

In the last few years, a number of new construction projects in Montreal have attempted to meet concerns about architectural preservation by saving parts of older buildings.

In addition to existing buildings constructed mostly in the late 1970s and 1980 that exemplify this attitude, such as Université du Québec à Montréal (UQAM) on St. Denis Street and Place Mercantile on Sherbrooke Street, many more are currently under construction or development today. They include Concordia University's new library on Bishop Street, the Montreal Museum of Fine Arts expansion on Sherbrooke Street, the Hôtel le Palais and the World Trade Centre, the latter two on St. Jacques Street.

For many purists in the preservation movement, façadism is the term used when only one or two of the exterior walls of a building are saved. They claim that such treatment desecrates a building. In many such cases, it is apparent that the architect and his client have taken the easy way out, paying lip service to preservation without really accepting the building in its surroundings.

Are there any cases when façadism is acceptable? With Montreal's typical row housing, gut rehabilitation of a house may remove everything inside, leaving only the greystone façade. In this case, it is only the occupants who are affected, deprived of the enjoyment of the original design.

Except for buildings whose interiors are of exceptional interest and whose original design is intact, this is not too grave a compromise since it maintains the character and appearance of the area. Heritage conservation often concerns itself only with exteriors, the parts of a building that are visible from the street.

Of course, in the case of certain exceptional buildings, often public in nature (e.g. banks, hotels and cinemas), property owners should be required to conserve the interiors. When the building interior maintains the original design intact or contains an impressive collection of decorative elements that would be difficult and/or costly to duplicate, there are reasons to preserve the interior as well.

Individuals interested more in urban design than heritage argue that preservation of façades may be acceptable in certain situations. In his seminal book, *Fundamentals of Urban Design*, Richard Hedman, long-time head of the urban design division of the City of San Francisco planning department, establishes a number of guidelines for acceptable conservation of building elements. It is interesting to evaluate recent Montreal buildings in terms of these principles:

— It is necessary to keep a sufficient depth of a building so that it retains the impression of being capable of independent use and appears structurally stable by itself.

UQAM's Judith-Jasmin building is undoubtedly the worst abuse of this concept: The soaring greystone bell tower of the former St. Jacques Cathedral appears ludicrous in front of the ponderous brick façades of the new building.

More acceptable is the plan to convert the Dominion Express building into part of the Hôtel le Palais (on St. Jacques). The most recent plan for the building indicated that two of the principal façades are to be preserved. Consequently, if it is completed as originally planned, only looking at the rear of the building will it be apparent that everything but the façades of the original structures has been eliminated.

Unfortunately, having accepted the principle of façadism, developers are tempted to rearrange a building's components as they like, with little respect for the original design. Modifications to the Hôtel le Palais project demonstrate this danger. Not content to merely avoid conserving the interior of the Dominion Express building, the developers now plan to dismantle the terra cotta ornaments on the corner of the building and reinstall them on top of two new storeys that will be added.

Adjacent to the Dominion Express building is the former Provincial Bank of Canada (221 St. Jacques Street) whose façade is intended to form an office and condominium building. Here is a case where it is unfortunate that the elaborate banking hall, typical of the sumptuous banks of the early 20th century, was not saved. This lofty interior space merited preservation. It might have become an interesting feature of the structure. Instead, some interior elements were sold off, the rest demolished in 1987.

Plans for the Concordia University library indicate that the Royal George apartment building will be surrounded by new construction the depth of the building will be visually truncated. The Royal George becomes a mere appendage, like ivy planted to mask unattractive design.

— Cantilevering or bridging out over a smaller building should be avoided because of the bizarre context in which the smaller building is placed. The scale differential tends to turn the original building into a kind of relic or curiosity.

The Centre Eaton/McGill College project, as originally conceived, ignored this advice. It was to include the construction of a 31-storey office tower on top of a portion of the City and District Savings Bank (McGill College Avenue at St. Catherine Street). Unless the structural overhang was done unobtrusively, it would make the 1933 bank look like a mere appendage. At publication time, the Centre Eaton was nearing completion, while the office tower was on hold.

Another example of this mistake was the original design for the project on the block occupied by the Queen's Hotel. The June 1988 site development plan (plan d'ensemble), which was to retain the oldest façades (subsequently demolished) would have had two 25-storey towers rising above the 19th-century red sandstone walls of the hotel. The promoters were able to convince the city planning department and the Ministry of Cultural Affairs that this was acceptable because the building had been shorn of its original fine interior during the years it stood vacant.

Of course, with the demolition, this project will never see the light of day. Will the preservation of the 1920s annex — consolation prize for the loss of the earlier structure — be as unappealing as the original design of the condominium complex? With the 1989 slump in the luxury condominium market, we may have to wait a while to find out. There has been no construction work on the Queen's Hotel site for more than a year.

The Place Mercantile office tower on Sherbrooke Street is out of scale with the greystones to which it is attached.
Photo by Bryan Demchinsky.

The Hôtel le Palais is being recycled out of the Dominion Express building of St. Jacques Street.
Photo by Bryan Demchinsky.

— Additions on the tops of buildings should not deform or adversely affect the composition of the façade, nor should the addition be out of scale with the building.

The Montreal World Trade Centre, where four-storey additions are to be built directly on top of façades of similar size, flies in the face of this advice. The architects argue that this will enhance the composition of the existing façade, the scale being modified in an acceptable way. While the architects' drawings seem quite attractive, reality may be quite different. It is an audacious design that cannot be judged until the buildings are completed.

— Surrounding buildings must create an appropriately scaled setting so as not to overwhelm or otherwise diminish the building's original streetscape role.

This is the rule broken by Place Mercantile on Sherbrooke Street. The row of greystone façades seems crushed by the 27-storey office tower to which it is attached. The buildings' original position on Sherbrooke Street has been severely compromised. Adding further to the strangeness of this group is the fact that the windows, which were originally divided into separate panes whose proportions and arrangement echoed the rhythm of the façade, have been replaced by single panes of glass creating an effect known as "little Orphan Annie eyes."

The preservation of two walls of the New Sherbrooke apartment building as part of the Montreal Museum of Fine Arts' new annex is open to criticism on a variation of this rule. The new building to which the New Sherbrooke will be attached is monumental in design, if not scale, creating an unappealing juxtaposition of new and old.

When taken to excess, the preservation of façades and other bits and pieces of a building is exploitive, akin to necrophilia. Present design requirements too often seek the rearrangement of an old structure, leading the contemporary architect to neglect the spirit of the original building. Instead of trying to improve the original architecture, it is more creative to try to find new uses and designs that respect the existing building.

Perhaps the best way to start is to examine the existing building in order to decide the scale of the new use planned. It is not impossible to sensitively convert an existing building to another use. For example, an

The greystone bell tower of the former St. Jacques Cathedral on St. Denis Street is an out-of-context appendage to the Université du Québec à Montréal's Judith Jasmin building. *Courtesy of The Gazette.*

The façade of the Royal George apartment building on Bishop Street will be surrounded by new construction in Concordia University's new library.

apartment building like the New Sherbrooke is made up of a series of small modules. When conversion of a public building like a museum or library is contemplated, the architect can take advantage of the fact that such institutions do require separate, smaller spaces for offices, study rooms, etc., in addition to large spaces for galleries and book stacks. The design could have small rooms surrounding the larger interior space to take advantage of the original appearance of the building. The fruits of this principle are evident in Maison Alcan, where executive offices are housed in the original houses along Sherbrooke Street, offering windows looking on to Sherbrooke Street as managerial perks.

The true challenge for architects working with existing buildings is to design a new structure with a new use while respecting the integrity of the original elements that are a part of it. It is one that few have met in Montreal.

The Four Lives of Pointe St. Charles

PIETER SIJPKES

Tightly hemmed in by the Lachine Canal, elevated railway tracks and the Canadian National marshalling yards, Pointe St. Charles resembles a mediaeval town encompassed by moats, walls and fortifications.

Carrying the analogy a step further, the elevated railway track that cuts the "quartier" into two roughly equal sections, resembles the traditional river that flows through most old towns. In Pointe St. Charles, the elevated track links Halifax with Vancouver, while the traditional river links the mountains with the sea; the bridges that channel life in the mediaeval town have become the d'Argenson, Charlevoix and Hibernia underpasses; the pedestrian underpass at Congrégation Street sometimes feels like one of those small doors that appear unexpectedly in massive fortifications.

Again, as in old towns, the church takes a central position in Pointe St. Charles: two massive greystone structures side by side facing Centre Street, the English Catholic church to the west, serving St. Gabriel parish, the French Catholic to the east, serving the parish of St. Charles. A lovely presbytery is conveniently squeezed in between, presumably staffed by bilingual priests. Other denominations such as Presbyterian, Methodist, Anglican, Ukrainian Catholic and Sikh are sprinkled along the lesser arteries the way the synagogues of Cordoba or the Protestant churches of Paris are dispersed.

The analogy of mediaeval splendour and Montreal's, if not Canada's, most romanticized squalor may seem iconoclastic, but a pattern is a pattern, as the architect Robert Venturi proclaimed when he published *Learning from Las Vegas*, in which he compares the plan and organization of the Nevada gambling mecca with the palace at Versailles.

If anyone were to search for a part of Canada that is representative of the whole country, this is it. Within its confined territory there are traces from the pre-colonial past, and a splendid farmhouse dating back to the time when the area was one big farm. The whole urban pattern is shaped by the 19th-century engineering works, while, most recently, residential development has been its single most important characteristic.

These unique qualities were revealed to my student-teammate Joe Carter and I when, in 1971, we walked every nook and cranny of the neighbourhood in order to draw the 3D view of the area, which he produced as part of an architectural assignment, and which now illustrates this essay.

Living in the area for the past dozen years has given me the opportunity to experience the walled-in quality of the place. To a great extent it explains why the residents feel such strong attachment to their turf: either you are a burgher of the Pointe or you are not, which means that at best you are from one of the faubourgs such as Verdun or Ville Emard or Côte St. Paul or Griffintown, or you come from faraway places such as Montreal or Westmount or the South Shore.

To be a fullblown "citoyen" one should certainly have been born here and preferably have a resident grandmother or two occupying one of the five old-age homes that dot the area. As some newly minted condo owners are finding out to their chagrin, length of stay counts. It is not only the physical layout that gives the place such an extraordinary sense of self — the long and eventful history that created the Pointe contributes to a large degree.

In its first incarnation, which I like to call its bucolic era, the Pointe must have been a good hunting and fishing ground, defined as it was in pre-colonial days by the St. Pierre River to the west (which now runs ungloriously through a culvert underneath Butler Street), the Little St. Pierre River to the north (where the Lachine Canal now slumbers) and the mighty St. Lawrence to the south (still there, but a lot tamer, channelled and dammed and regulated as it is.)

To get an idea of what life was like, Cartier's description of his first visit to Hochelaga on October 2, 1535, can't be beat: "And on reaching Hochelaga, there came to meet us more than a thousand persons, both men and women and children who gave us as good a welcome as ever a father gave to his son, making great signs of joy; for the men danced in one ring, the women in another and the children also apart by themselves. After this they brought us quantities of fish, and of their bread which is made of Indian corn, throwing so much of it into our longboats that it seemed to rain bread."

It took another century before Montreal was founded, on May 18 1642, at Pointe à Callières where the St. Pierre River joined the St. Lawrence. Pointe St. Charles was soon after turned into farmland, which became the area's second vocation.

"Shall I rip my mother's breast?" is the reported gasp of one Indian upon seeing a plow for the first time. Rip the newcomers did, as is testified by the magnificent Ferme St. Gabriel, built in 1698, which is the best preserved historic building in Montreal from that era. It has unfortunately been cut off from its river frontage by tracks and the Bonaventure expressway, and has been overwhelmed on the north side by ill-conceived low-rent housing blocks built in the early 1950s, but with the help of a foggy day it is fun to imagine this building, on the edge of the river, solitary, surrounded by fields.

The deterioration of the relationship of the newly arrived French colonists and the natives can be gleaned from a marble plaque affixed to the fire station at the corner of Richmond and Richardson Streets: "Ici fut le fort St. Gabriel et près d'ici le père Le Maistre fut Massacré par les Iroquois en embuscade. 26 Aout 1661." Whereas père Le Maistre was done in by the Iroquois, Fort St. Gabriel fell victim to the forces of progress without leaving a trace.

The Lachine massacre of 1686 is not only another example of the less than friendly relations between the "nouveaux arrivés" and the native population; it also put to an end the first attempt to bypass the Lachine rapids with a canal. Lack of funds was already hampering the attempt by Montreal's first civil engineer, Dollier de Casson, but the massacre put a definitive end to his effort. It was not until 1825 that the first Lachine Canal was opened with great pomp and circumstance, heralding the end of the agricultural era of the Pointe and the beginning of its third life: industry and transportation were taking over where nuns, cows and corn had reigned supreme.

While peddling along the present Lachine Canal bike path, it is hard to imagine that this murky ditch was at one time the only Canadian link between the interior of the North American continent and the outside world, but there it is, our watery umbilical cord.

The building of the canal occupied thousands of workers, particularly French Canadians and recently arrived Irish immigrants. Their working conditions were harsh, as is brought out by the testimony tabled by the committee formed to investigate the violent strike of 1837, when the canal was being enlarged. Wages of a few dollars a week, strife between French Canadian and Irish workers, long layoffs and dismissals without cause were listed as the main reasons for the eruption of violence. The persistent elements of life in Pointe St. Charles were emerging: a mixed French and Irish population, hard work for little pay, little or no security, and stubborn pride.

However convenient and progressive the new canal may have been at the time, its hegemony was already challenged by the newfangled railway when the second enlargement was finished in 1848. Whereas the canal only skirted the northern edge of the Pointe, the railway would soon encircle it and slice it in half; the smoke of the engines would darken the sky and soot would cover every surface. The Montreal-Lachine railroad had been opened in 1847, directly competing for freight with the skippers, while the ambition to link Montreal with an ice-free harbour led to a proposal by local and British industrialists (as they were called in those days) to build a line linking Montreal to Portland, Maine. To that end a bridge across the St. Lawrence was required. The Victoria Bridge, the biggest engineering feat of the British Empire, was designed and prefabricated in England and shipped across the ocean, every angle iron and plate and rivet of it, and erected by the same mix of French Canadians and Irishmen that had worked on the Lachine Canal. Spanning the St. Lawrence from the eastern edge of the Pointe two miles across to St. Lambert, it was originally planned to hit the South Shore farther down stream; Centre Street in Pointe St. Charles was at one time just a survey line for the axis of the projected bridge. At the Pointe end of the bridge there still stands one of the most moving monuments of that period. Immortalized by William Notman's photographic eye, the Irish workers on the bridge haul an almost magical black stone out of the river, which they erected and inscribed: "TO PRESERVE FROM DESECRATION THE REMAINS OF 6,000 IMMIGRANTS WHO DIED OF SHIP FEVER A.D. 1847–8 THIS STONE IS ERECTED BY THE WORKMEN OF MESS'RS PETO, BRASSEY & BETTS EMPLOYED IN THE CONSTRUCTION OF THE VICTORIA BRIDGE A.D. 1859.

When the Prince of Wales presided over the official opening ceremonies of the bridge in 1860 and made an inaugural trip over, or rather through it, the flaws of the structure became all too apparent: built as a

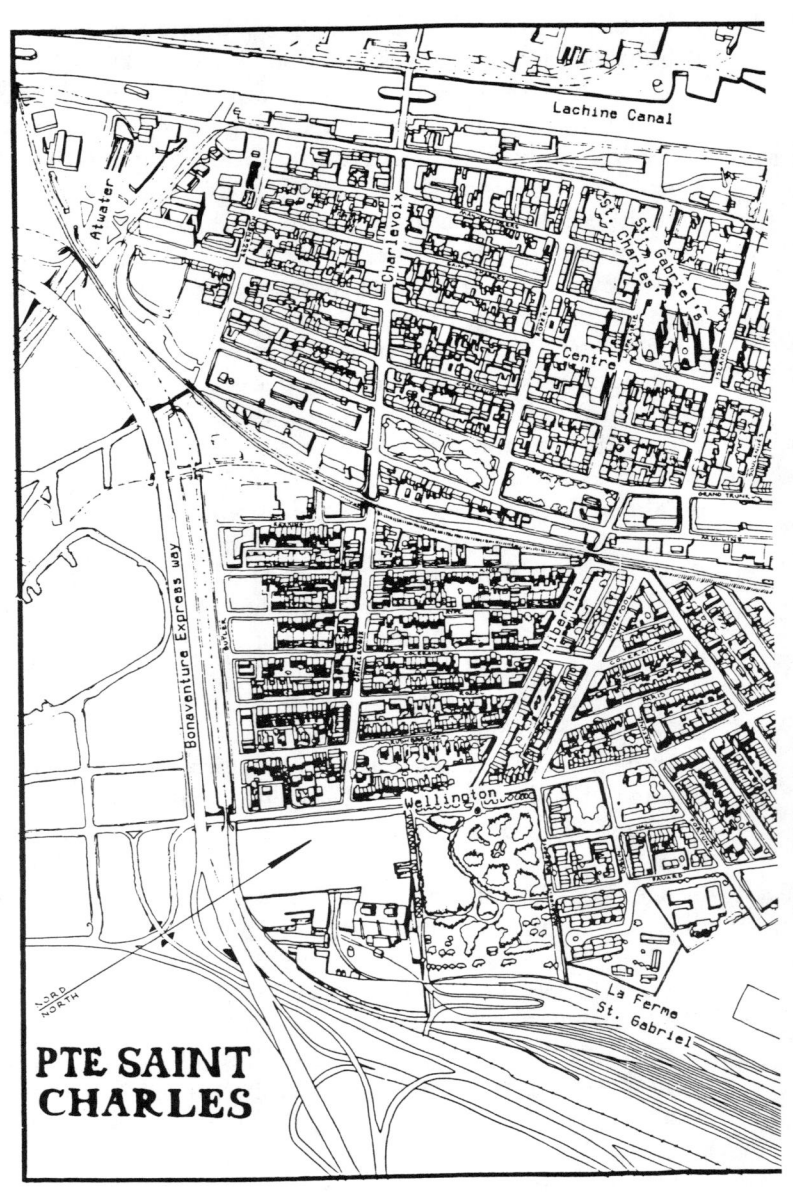

*Courtesy of Pieter Sijpkes and Joe Carter,
McGill School of Architecture.*

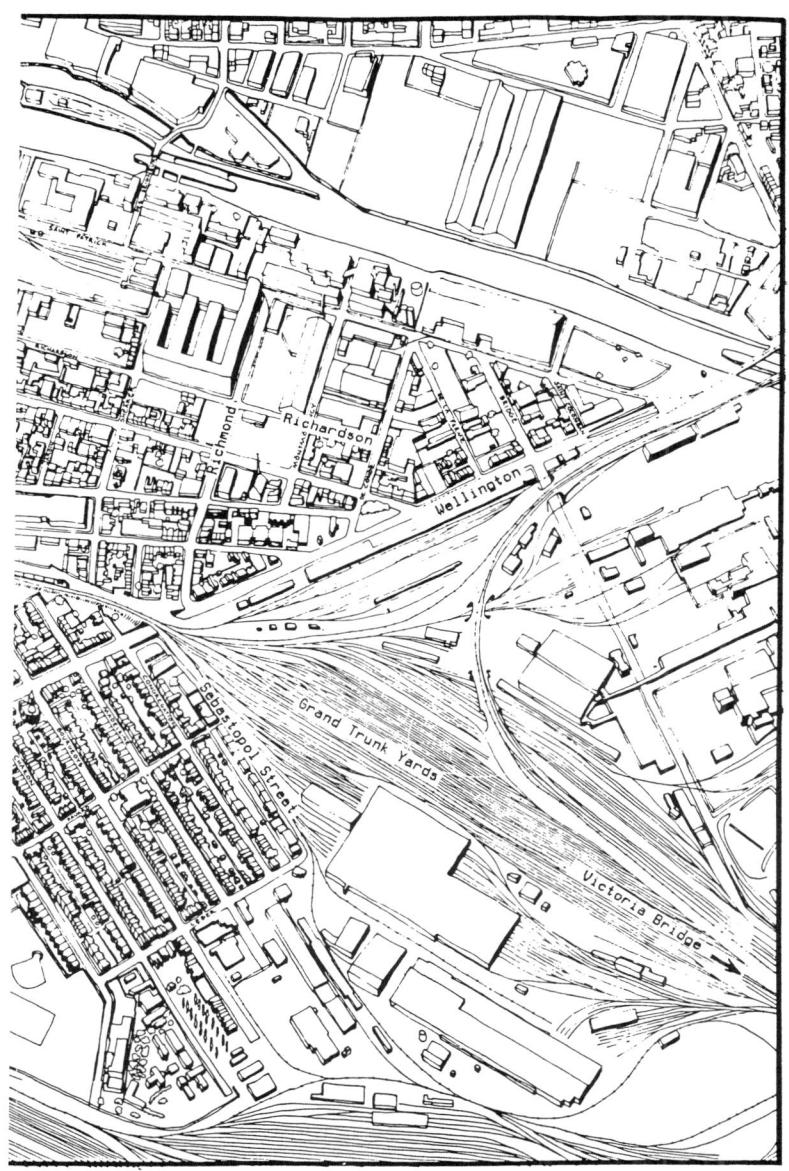

tube with a single track inside, the prince and his entourage were very nearly suffocated by the time they emerged at St. Lambert. Foreshadowing other Montreal mega-projects, the bridge was opened late and was much more expensive than anticipated. The tube was taken down in 1898 and replaced by the open-lattice structure that still sits on the original stone piers. A beautiful volume illustrated with plans, construction details and erection procedures was issued by the contractors as was customary in Victorian days. A section of the tube, even a reconstructed one, would be a suitable monument to this first bridge across the St. Lawrence.

It was not only the building of the bridge that brought activity and development to the Pointe: a terminus building, the marshalling yards and the Grand Trunk engine shops were all constructed at the eastern side of the district. In a few years, this part of the district was transformed from a farm into the centre of Canadian industry.

On Sebastopol Street still stands a dilapidated row of red brick flats, built by and for the employees of the bridge contractors: Canada's first industrial workers' housing. Built of solid masonry, featuring sloped roofs and stacked dwellings, this humble row, if restored, would make a most appropriate setting for a museum, documenting workers lives in the Victorian era. Facing squarely onto the marshalling yards, as they always have, these flats embody the utilitarian nature of residential planning in all of Pointe St. Charles. Streets such as Congrégation, Ste. Madeleine, Bourgeois, Charron and Ash, (collectively nicknamed Soweto — South of Wellington), laid out and constructed in the 1860s and early 1870s, follow the pattern initiated on Sebastopol.

Houses or flats face the sidewalk squarely with little or no setback and are provided with relatively generous yards to allow for an outdoor privy as well as a small garden. Access to the yard is either provided by a porte-cochere (carriage entrance) or by an alley, whichever way the small speculators found more profitable. On Ste. Madeleine Street my rowhouse is part of a block of eight units put up in 1877 by a Dr. Desjardins, while eight units across the street were financed by his wife.

The alley serving the yards abruptly stops mid-block; the rest of the houses are provided with porte-cocheres; garbage collecting has been confusing on this street ever since. As I found out, construction standards were minimal at the time; the myth of the high quality of construction in the "olden days" has been laid to rest by many renovators, often at great expense. The design recipe throughout called for a flat brick façade, set on a narrow rubble foundation, standard windows cut sharply, balconies and entrance porches protruding in wood, the whole capped by a cornice that might show some decoration.

It is exactly this minimalist quality that unifies the whole district and highlights the elaborateness of the occasional ornate church or bank or fire station. It is too bad that a lot of renovation now going on does not respect this simple pattern: windows are introduced of all kinds of sizes, cornices are removed and sheet metal creeps across the façades of the district. (The rear of the buildings has been sheet-metal land for decades; the alley landscape is fundamentally different from the streetscape.)

In this area water was initially supplied by a common well at Favard Street. Renovators might pause when they install their tubs, microwaves and fax machines and remember that their newly insulated and gyprocked flats started out with a brick chimney as the only service device, used for heating as well as for cooking.

The almost annual flooding that plagued not only Pointe St. Charles but all the low lying areas in the region occasionally made for living conditions that may well have inspired Charles Dickens when he spent some time in Montreal.

It definitely did inspire Herbert Ames Brown, around the turn of the century, to write *The City Below the Hill,* the first critical essay on living conditions of workers in the Pointe St. Charles and St. Henri districts. He went as far as putting up a model housing project in Griffintown, which unfortunately no longer exists.

Unlike the industrial town of Pullman outside of Chicago, or the railway neighbourhood in Sydenham in England, or scores of other industrial towns, the development of Pointe St. Charles was ad hoc, without a grand urban vision. The streets were laid out to fit the parcels of land left between the tracks, or crossed the canal at the locks, as is the case at Seigneurs Street.

Only Wellington Street, that old dirt track linking Old Montreal with Lachine and points beyond, is a remnant of the days when a road followed the ground contours; too bad there is not a trace left of the tollhouse that stood where Hibernia Street now starts. De la Ferme Street still exists to bear witness to the passing of the farm era — its short extent is now lined with dilapidated light industrial buildings.

However haphazardly the area's layout came about, it does inscribe on the landscape the human condition that was prevalent: the needs of industry and engineering first, those of the worker, at best, in second place. Seen from that perspective, Pointe St. Charles as a whole is a more accurate Museum of Civilization, certainly of the Victorian working man, than the recently opened edifice in Ottawa which seems to rely to a large degree on fibreglass mock-ups.

The era from the beginning of this century until the late 1950s was the industrial heyday of the Pointe. The infrastructure was complete; work, with the exception of the Depression years, was plentiful and the population reached a peak of about 35,000 souls, housed in overcrowded flats and tenements. When a large segment of the movie *Les Plouffes* was being filmed on Hibernia Street and some side streets, the only things that needed to be changed to bring the street back to the 1930s was the reintroduction of the street car and changing the street lights and advertising billboards.

It was again a major development in transportation that led ultimately to the Pointe's fourth calling. The replacement of the Lachine Canal with the St. Lawrence Seaway in 1959 was a double blow. Not only did shipping-related activities sharply diminish and finally cease altogether with the gradual closing of the canal, but the industry that had for a hundred years lined it also became obsolete and moved away. Redpath Sugar, Northern Electric, Belding Corticelli, Stelco Steel, Ogilvy Mills — the empty hulks of cranes, conveyors and silos stand empty and abandoned.

In addition, the general decline of railway activity in Canada has greatly reduced the level of activity at the former Grand Trunk (now Canadian National) shops. Over the last 25 years the population of the Pointe has declined to about 13,000 people. Of course, it was not only here that decline occurred; Victoriaville (or Goose Village), once a thriving community just east of the Victoria Bridge is now a dusty plain with zero inhabitants. Griffintown at the Montreal side of the Wellington tunnel is now mainly a light industrial area, housing only a handful of residents. These two communities were wiped out by a declining demand for their industries and thoughtless zoning practices on the part of the municipal administration.

The Pointe was saved by its mediaeval, self-contained layout and by its scrappy inhabitants who, in the late 1960s became probably the most organized community in Montreal, if not in Canada.

It was in the Pointe that housing renovation was first tried on a large scale. "Loge Peuple" was the first non-profit housing cooperative in Canada to take advantage of the financing offered by various levels of

The Victoria Bridge under construction
in 1859. It was the engineering feat
of the 19th century in Montreal.
Notman Photographic Archives.

Built in 1698, Ferme St. Gabriel is a vestige
of Pointe St. Charles' colonial period.
Shane Kelley, The Gazette.

A typical Pointe St. Charles
corner house on Hibernia Street.
Photo by Pieter Sijpkes.

A view of the Lachine Canal from the Seigneurs
Street locks. A revitalized canal area is part of a
new chapter in Pointe St. Charles' history.
Photo by Pieter Sijpkes.

government which allowed residents to buy their houses or flats, renovate them and rent them back to themselves at cost. Pointe St. Charles was in the forefront when the first experiments were carried out with community medical, legal and architectural clinics. Its Librairie Populaire predated the first City of Montreal library in the area by almost a decade.

The installation of the city library solved another problem in an innovative way: instead of tearing down the 1896 fire station in some misconceived scheme to widen Hibernia Street, local protest resulted in the then unheard of solution of installing the library in the renovated fire station.

The decline of industry, transportation and population has in a sense laid bare the social as well as physical structure of the place, the way the sun bleaches a skeleton in the desert. The black bridges over the canal, once sliding and turning and lifting themselves out of the way of the canal boats are now welded immobile, their superstructures ripped off, spans replaced by inglorious garbage fill. The locks, instead of kinematic and hydraulic marvels, are now just dumb corks holding the water back. The factories, once spewing smoke and soot, now stand mute and empty. The industrial and transportation era is definitely over.

The fourth life of Pointe St. Charles has again been brought about by revolutions in transportation. The opening of the Lachine Canal bicycle path recognized the importance of cycling as a serious mode of transportation and recreation. The path is a minor miracle and a major blessing. The miracle is that the canal was not filled in and asphalted over to bring yet more cars to downtown Montreal; the blessing is that it has allowed, on a nice Sunday, up to 50,000 Montrealers to leisurely enjoy the stark beauty of the canal zone and discover its communities such as Pointe St. Charles, Verdun and St. Henri.

The other revolution was the opening of the Charlevoix Métro Station. Surreptitious entry into fortress Pointe St. Charles is now commonplace: no more need to enter through the barriers of underpasses and bridges. The Charlevoix Métro swallows and regurgitates its passengers as do the other stations of the network.

The bicycle and the Métro have demolished the fortifications, and a stream of newcomers who before had never set foot in the Pointe has settled there. The conversion of the fire station into the library is now being followed by turning factories into condominiums. Sturdy names such as Stelco, Belding Corticelli, and soon Redpath, sound as good for pioneering condo projects as they did originally. In addition, the hundreds of empty lots created over the years by fires and abandonment are now being meticulously filled in with new construction, fixing the streetlines the way orthodontists fix smiles. The fourth career of the Pointe, that of an interesting residential neighbourhood, has begun.

The remnants of the previous vocations are still around, for those who wish to see them, the way mediaevalists can tell stories by looking at battle-scarred walls and redoubts. The dangers that lurk now are not the stealthy Iroquois of the 17th century, or the self-serving industrialists of the 19th century or the often greedy absentee landlords of the 20th century — the danger now lies in the obliteration of the social and physical heritage of the district.

In an unusually intense way, Pointe St. Charles has been a microcosm of Canada since its founding. It is here, of necessity, where bilingualism was the norm, where toleration was the norm, where cooperation was the norm, when wealthier parts of the country could indulge in their much narrower agendas. The new, more socially diversified community that is now forming inside the old "bourg" can only benefit from honouring this legacy, which shaped the very fabric of Pointe St. Charles.

HOUSING

While much attention is given to the Montreal's large development projects, the issue of where we live remains of fundamental importance.

If Montreal, in particular the inner city, is to remain a good place to live, ways must be found to revitalize areas affected by economic decline and to repair the damage done by outmoded methods of urban renewal.

Fortunately, there is reason for optimism. Montreal has escaped the worst effects of inner city population loss that has plagued other North American cities, and in recent years much new building in residential areas has been of high architectural quality, sensitive to traditional building patterns and respectful of the city's history.

Downtown Housing: Filling in the Gaps

IAN MACBURNIE

As part of its preliminary master plan released in 1988, the city presented policies intended to strengthen the vitality of the central area by increasing its residential population. To do this will require the construction of thousands of new housing units, as well as the conversion to housing of underused or obsolete industrial and commercial properties.

Montreal's central area, a region encompassing over 1,500 hectares, and incorporating 18 administrative districts including the commercial core, is currently home to some 60,000 residents. These districts are distinguishable, one from the next, by the wide disparities in their social and economic composition as well as by their particular urban and architectural characteristics.

The residential neighbourhoods to the west and north of the commercial core are almost entirely built up with few available sites remaining, and they are considered to be economically prosperous. The municipal government will therefore concentrate its efforts in the areas to east of Bleury Street (as far as Berri Street) and south of St. Antoine Street, sectors where vacant land is abundant.

Because of their proximity to a relatively healthy downtown, these districts should not, in theory, be fragmented. Historically, they contained small-scale, low-rent residential and commercial buildings which, by and large, successfully provided for the needs of their inhabitants.

But they have undergone a cataclysmic metamorphosis as a result of the enormous outward expansion and dramatic relocation of Montreal's traditional business and retailing centre. Following the construction of massive new office developments in the central core, accompanied by mass transit corridors, the landscape of southern and eastern districts was irrevocably altered. Coupled with land speculation on a massive scale, many of the area's as yet unredeveloped properties were purchased, their occupants dislocated, and their buildings demolished. Referred to as development parcels and either left derelict or operated as parking lots, these sites inevitably would be held off the market until the speculator was guaranteed a huge profit from the development of a large commercial real estate project.

Having directly encouraged such actions as an outcome of its laissez-faire, pro-redevelopment policies for the areas, the Drapeau administration, in pursuit of ever-enhanced tax revenues, was more than willing to sacrifice these districts, content to regard the inner-city areas not as communities, but rather as commodities.

To the great consternation of government and the real estate industry, this cavalier attitude towards the inner-city eventually backfired. As Montreal's once robust economy began to sputter and eventually stagnate in the 1970s and early 1980s, and as commercial real estate investment went elsewhere, districts east and south were abandoned in a state reminiscent of a ghost town. They are now socio-economically and physically decayed and without intervention will likely remain urban wastelands.

As regrettable as historical circumstances have been, it finally appears that regeneration of these inner-city neighbourhoods may be at hand. The current Montreal Citizens' Movement (MCM) administration, recognizing the need for action and realizing that economic and political realities rule out the city building significant quantities of housing on its own, has decided to implement programs that will stimulate private-sector construction of affordable housing. It is a laudable concept in theory, but an enormously difficult one to devise and implement. There are many important issues to consider.

First, the administration will need to create strategies that establish a mutually advantageous working relationship with the residential development industry.

To date, the city's experience as a partner with private builders has shown that neither the creation of truly affordable housing, nor the anticipated benefits of revitalization have occurred. The resulting programs up until now have offered nothing more sophisticated than the simple exchange of government-owned land for the provision of new inner-city housing.

Inner-city projects developed under Opération 20,000 logements, the city's former high-profile housing partnership, are a case in point. For many complex reasons, the previous administration was unable to persuade residential builders to incorporate a healthy mix of uses and functions in their projects. Preferring not to increase their risk by building commercial space, and entirely uninterested in including social and cultural facilities, builders erected block after block of sterile, mono-functional, low-rise, low-density, middle income condominium dwellings.

In disadvantaged inner-city districts such as St. Henri, it became clear that these projects callously disregarded the needs and aspirations of the area's existing residents and neglected the neighbourhood at large. Not surprisingly, this housing failed to stimulate regeneration of the areas in which it was built. More often than not, it resulted in the creation of segregated residential islands, isolated encampments to be inhabited by an outside elite. As the new residents preferred to shop and entertain elsewhere, the only people who benefited were the property speculators.

Land-for-housing partnerships like Opération 20,000 logements, although appropriate when initiated in the relatively uncomplicated peripheral suburbs, have proven singularly ineffective when used in the inner city. In light of this, the MCM administration must find a new partnership arrangement that indeed creates affordable housing while stimulating inner-city regeneration.

A second problem to be solved has its roots in demographic trends that indicate an alarming decrease in the region-wide population growth. It remains to be seen whether the value of the environmentally deteriorated inner-city districts can be increased sufficiently to attract a sufficient number of new residents.

Fortunately, there is cause for optimism. Undertaking a much more thorough analysis of the condition of inner-city districts, the administration has determined that areas east and south are characterized by two distinctly separate yet classifiable sets of conditions. It has concluded that these sectors can be designated as belonging to either a revitalization or a development district. This distinction is the first step, and an extremely important one, towards the creation of individually tailored initiatives. Programs using the area-specific approach have been employed with

Economic decline and projects such as the
Ville Marie expressway have left southern and western
parts of downtown with plenty of parking space.
Photo by Len Sidaway, The Gazette.

The Faubourg des Récollets district west of McGill Street
is one of the areas that has been targetted for redevelopment.
Photo by Ian MacBurnie.

considerable success in cities as diverse as Berlin and Glasgow. Vast areas of their inner cities, devastated by war in the case of Berlin and by industrial decline in Glasgow, were redeveloped into thriving mixed-use communities.

In Montreal, neighbourhoods such as St. Laurent, between St. Laurent Boulevard and St. Denis below Sherbrooke Street, and Faubourg des Récollets have been designated as revitalization districts. They still contain a significant number of buildings, though vacant sites are prevalent. Typically, although sharing certain similarities they are sufficiently different, one from the next, that no two possess identical problems. Generally, land in these districts is owned either by large land speculators, as in the case of the Faubourg des Récollets, or by individual entrepreneurs, as in St. Laurent.

To date, unilateral private-sector development has not occurred. Reasons include the incompatibility of land uses, the high cost of building conversion, the difficulty of land assembly, the presence of restrictive or non-conforming zoning, and uncertain market potential.

Development districts, on the other hand, are generally as such classified because of the presence of vast tracts of derelict land resulting from uncontrolled speculation, planning blight or the loss of a previous usage. Represented by sectors such as Place des Arts, Bleury-Dorchester, Bonaventure and Faubourg Québec (the mostly vacant area along Notre Dame Street immediately to the east of Old Montreal), development districts are characterized by their sheer extent; so great, in fact, that they present the opportunity to create entirely new neighbourhoods. Development zones, although classifiably similar, possess significant differences depending upon their size, location, and whether or not vestiges of their resident populations still survive.

Generally, land in development districts is controlled by one of two groups: a level of government or the city's new housing and urban development corporation (SHDM), as in the case of Bonaventure and the Faubourg Québec, or by large scale, well-entrenched land speculators, as in the case of Place des Arts and Bleury-Dorchester. Unilateral private-sector development has not occurred here either because the sector's proximity to the financial core has forced the price of land to exceed the residential market potential, or bureaucratic intransigence has resulted in repeated delays in the redevelopment of government-controlled property.

To revalorize these areas, the city must adopt a high-profile, interventionist role in the redevelopment of individual districts. To this end, it will have to prepare, preferably with local area participation, district by district master plans that would take into account the specific hindrances to new housing investment. To ensure these areas develop individual identities of sufficient quality to compete with older, established neighbourhoods, the administration will need to prepare local area urban design guidelines. These should be developed to reinforce each district's particular assets, as well as to anticipate the nature and location of the social and cultural amenities essential for the creation of well-balanced communities. They should also determine the typologies and morphologies of future affordable housing projects.

It will also be necessary to establish a significant land bank, to be built up by assuming control of land already owned by various levels of government, and through the expropriation of key tracts of property in both revitalization and development districts.

To encourage private-sector participation, the city should designate these areas as priority development districts and market them aggressively. This tactic would raise their profile, identifying them as unique investment opportunities. In addition, making available special economic and development benefits would go a long way towards negating their high-risk image. Negotiating with prospective developers on a project-by-project basis, the administration would be able to offer as incentive financial and development credits for housing that provided significant benefits for either the sector's existing residents or businesses.

Finally, the city must recognize from the outset the necessity of investing tens of millions of dollars in projects such as the creation of schools and parks, and the redesign of existing roadways and infrastructure. The high cost will mean a creative approach to financing, one that will likely involve a complex system of development-package linkages with major, up-market commercial and residential developments of the type undertaken elsewhere in the commercial core.

One can only hope that this time around, the right vision will initiate the right action. As Italo Calvino writes: "Futures not achieved are only branches of the past. Dead branches."

Housing That Belongs on Montreal Streets

ADRIAN SHEPPARD

By and large, the course of Montreal's recent development is not a happy one. To a great extent, the city is cluttered up with buildings devoid of any sense of place. They are designed by architects who are oblivious to the city's form and traditions, for patrons who lack an architectural or urban culture.

Most critics will argue that the struggle for survival of the downtown is already lost, that the core is fast becoming a lifeless collage of over-sized "complexes," where middle-income housing can no longer be sustained.

Fortunately for Montreal (and for the more responsible members of its architectural community), the picture is not entirely bleak. Sprinkled throughout the island are a significant number of recently completed low-to medium-cost housing projects that stand as examples of good urban architecture. These new developments clearly break away from the monotonous trend of either banal or egocentric buildings that have come to characterize the city's centre. They fit the definition of architecture as "culturally responsible building," because they integrate well with neighbouring buildings and respect the social and historical context of city streets as well as their traditional forms. It has been Montreal's fate to have been either too poor or too conservative in its urban attitudes to succumb radically to the Modernist transfiguration in public housing. The tradition of the small-scale housing development, at ease in the traditional city street, has not been entirely lost. In fact, some critics point out that Montreal's most important contribution to urban architecture in recent years lies precisely in the realm of public housing.

The purpose of this essay is to examine the unsung heroes of Montreal architecture in terms of their urban and cultural relevance and in terms of their ability to build upon or repair the urban fabric. The common denominator in these projects is the willingness to sustain, rather than oppose, existing lifestyles and the conscious desire to be dependent on the physical or cultural circumstances of which they are a part.

To have a critical appreciation of local architecture one must have an understanding of the ordering ideas and the formal structure of the city. The traditional well-balanced urban environment was made up of clearly defined open spaces that were contained and supported by a continuous low-profile, medium-density building fabric. These spaces constituted a hierarchy of interrelated squares, streets, parks and gardens. The fabric itself was made up of a large number of background buildings and relatively few foreground buildings. The background buildings, which gave the city its texture, contained the more private and anonymous functions; they included offices, places of commerce and most of the housing. The foreground buildings, those that made the urbanistic statements, housed the socially more significant functions, and included churches and major civic buildings. This close interdependence between buildings and spaces, between background and foreground, provided the urban environment with a hierarchical order. It enabled the city to have its landmarks and focal points stand as visible counterpoints to the neutral urban tissue. It gave the city an obvious clarity.

Modernism, as an architectural and planning ideology, has literally reversed this order. The sense of hierarchy has been jettisoned. The buildings have taken precedence over the spaces. The free-standing building, conceived as sculpted object, is favoured over the contiguous ones. The largest buildings are no longer the most significant ones, and the most significant ones are not the best. Few public buildings attain landmark status and many that ought to be relegated to the rank of fabric, posture for attention.

Fortunately, the pendulum is beginning to swing back the other way. The focus of current architectural debate is shifting from the importance of the individual building to that of the relationship of building to city, city to culture and city to history. The examples discussed in this study, have been chosen precisely because they embody this new, yet very traditional, attitude about the city: that an urban building is an integral part of a larger organism, the city, and that it derives its meaning from the relationship it establishes with its context.

For the most part, Montreal's housing stock was built by small developers producing relatively modest-scale projects that responded quite accurately to the needs and cultural habits of its occupants. A 10-to-20-dwelling unit project was the norm, too small to upset the urban ecology in a radical way, but large enough to have a presence. David Hanna, an urban geographer who has studied the history of housing in Montreal, convincingly explains the reasons for and the benefits of a cyclical and small-scale housing industry. The well-defined construction cycles throughout the city's history, together with the relatively modest size of development ventures, shaped our city and gave it an immense variety in housing. This diversity relates equally to the typology as to the architectural expression of the housing.

In more recent times, Montreal has not been spared from the violent intrusion of large housing projects such as the Rockhill Apartments, La Cité, Place Frontenac and Fort de la Montagne. Nevertheless, these have been relatively few compared to other North American cities. The local market conditions and the nature of the building industry have maintained the tradition of the modest-size housing developments. Non-corporate housing developers as well as the small contracting firms specializing in housing are still common. This has been particularly evident in the realm of public housing, where a marked effort has been made by municipal authorities to sustain the tradition and to encourage the fragmentation of large projects. It has been the case even where economic considerations or needs warrant the construction of large projects.

The story of Montreal's public housing began in earnest in 1942 with the construction of La Cité Jardin du Tricentenaire, northeast of Maisonneuve Park near the Olympic Village. The project originally called for 500 units, but was aborted after 168 houses were completed. Unlike all its successors it contained only detached dwelling units; there were to be no multiple-unit residential blocks. Cité Jardin remains today one of the most successful Canadian applications of the Radburn plan, a 1920s garden-city concept developed by Clarence Stein and based on a premise of segregation of auto traffic and pedestrian movement within residential districts. It was a significant project, but one that stood somewhat apart from the rest of the city, and it had no real follow-up.

Les Habitations Jeanne-Mance, found along de Maisonneuve Boulevard a block east of St. Laurent Boulevard, was completed in the mid-1950s. It was the city's first significant and largest-ever public housing project built in the city centre. It was imposed on the municipality by the provincial government of Maurice Duplessis, who defined its form, scope and location. Jean Drapeau was violently opposed to the project, but was unable to stop it. Ironically, Drapeau, the man who later came to rally behind so many large-scaled projects, including the Olympic Village, stated at the time that we had entered the Nuclear Age and that in the event of a nuclear war, it would be nearly impossible to evacuate the inhabitants from the proposed towers in an efficient manner. Public housing was the exclusive jurisdiction of the province. In fact, the city administration did not even include a housing authority.

The project, designed by Greenspoon, Freedlander and Dunne, with Rother, Bland and Trudeau acting as planning consultants, stood at the time for progressive urban renewal. Les Habitations Jeanne-Mance conformed to a simple planning formula that had an impeccable, albeit limited logic: the quality of life within a neighbourhood has more to do with the quantity of light, sunshine, greenspace and level of hygiene than with traditional urban values. Thus, renewal as an urban regeneration process, began with a radical clearing of the site; then the old "quartier" is replaced with what is essentially a park, in which are deposited a number of low linear blocks interspersed with a few high towers to compensate for the low density of the low-profile buildings. There are no more fronts and no more backs to the buildings, there are no more lanes, there are no more streets, there are no more private or semi-private outdoor spaces. It is, in short, the embodiment of a heroic but fundamentally anti-urban vision.

Although the city was to wait until 1967 to have its own housing authority, Le Service d'habitation de Montréal, it had already started in 1965 to negotiate with the province for greater autonomy in the field of housing.

When Petite-Bourgogne, the second public-housing project of importance, was started in 1966, the responsibility for its design and management was given to the city. Not unlike Les Habitations Jeanne-Mance, it was perceived at first as a "conventional" urban renewal project of magnitude. However, the city quickly rejected the "tabula rasa" strategy used in the planning of Les Habitations Jeanne-Mance and adopted a gentler attitude toward the insertion of new buildings in an older neighbourhood; an attempt would be made to maintain and repair the

La Cité Jardin du Tricentenaire, built in 1942,
was Montreal's first public housing project.
Photo by Adrian Sheppard.

Les Habitations de Grand Pré Street is small "a"
architecture at its finest, in keeping with the building
styles of Montreal and integrated into the neighbourhood.
Photo by Adrian Sheppard.

While remaining an affirmation of modernity,
Parc Quesnel remains contextually meaningful.
Photo by Adrian Sheppard.

Les Habitations Jeanne-Mance was the only 'large-scale'
urban renewal project undertaken in Montreal.
Courtesy of The Gazette.

urban fabric and to rehabilitate as many dwelling units as possible. The designers, Ouellet, Reeves and Allain, were no doubt conscious of urban theories about connections between old and new parts of the city and about sympathetic attitudes toward older neighbourhoods. Most importantly, the city would reduce the scale of the project from 800 to 315 dwelling units. But because of its visibility, its scale and its marked delineation, Petite-Bourgogne is still perceived by its inhabitants and outsiders alike as an isolated entity, a ghetto in the city.

Petite-Bourgogne was the first child of the Service d'habitation, but it was actually, while undertaking its second venture, Opération 300 logements, (this project was unrelated to later housing programs Opération 10,000 logements and Opération 20,000 logements) that the city finally set the tone and defined a policy for future housing developments. Guy Legault, the service's first director and its guiding light, reduced, once again, the scale of the project (completed in 1969) by fragmenting it into four 75-unit developments and located these in four unrelated neighbourhoods of the city.

This process of small-scale interventions, virtually always on vacant land, continues today. Each project becomes an opportunity for urban repair and constituted a humane manner of implanting social housing in the city.

Les Habitations Notre-Dame, by Mercier, Boyer and Mercier, stands as one of the better illustrations of this dual-purpose mission: that of providing "background" public housing and of repairing or consolidating a damaged urban fabric. The project, located along Notre Dame Street, east and west of Viau Street, is nearly completed and includes 75 low-cost dwelling units spread over 11 separate sites, all of which are "residues" of expropriation for the construction of the Ville Marie expressway. When the expressway was built, a series of adjacent city blocks were decapitated. These blocks literally lost what is commonly referred to as their "tête d'îlot," the end building that gives the street its urban façade and shields the semi-public inner space and the service lane from public viewing.

The project was conceived as a re-completion of the city blocks with a series of triplexes, not very different from those of the neighbourhood, but different enough in their architectural language to set them apart from their predecessors and to express unequivocally their variances of scale, program and construction. These buildings speak of Montreal, of its block morphology and of its occupants.

Not all the good examples of this new architecture fall within the realm of public or social housing. Les Cours Sainte-Famille, built in 1984 and designed by Cayouette and Saïa, is one of the most successful medium-cost inserts in a tight urban street. Its expression is frankly contemporary despite the fact that this project is more concerned with the issue of urban continuity than with its own strictly functional requirements. The project is built around a private internal courtyard that gives it a unique sense of place, without in any way dissociating itself from the street of which it is a part. When compared to the adjacent Victorian houses, the project is tight and compact, but a comfortable addition to Ste. Famille Street.

Two other private-sector projects, developed and designed by Dan Hanganu, on Nuns' Island, are possibly the best and most credible illustrations that good housing can be both contemporary and contextual. Although both were built on undeveloped land away from the city's centre, these townhouse projects have a distinct urban character. The first project, on de Gaspé Street, designed in 1980, was Hanganu's first venture in housing of that type. Without being an actual copy of any housing in the city, this project embodies and continues a well-established Montreal housing vocabulary of double-hung windows, elevated and protected main entry, predominant verticality, wood construction with masonry mitoyen walls and ornamented brick veneer. While the units depart from the traditional row-house, they nevertheless constitute correct responses to conditions of site, living style and market in their use of centrally located stairs, rear living room and small level changes in the floor.

Hanganu's project on Corot Street, dating from about the same time, is possibly Montreal's most elegant contemporary housing complex. Like its sister project, it is a terrace of townhouses built on vacant land, but in this case, overlooking the St. Lawrence River. Despite its relatively low overall density, the row of houses has a vigorous street presence. Here one finds no reference to the traditional Montreal housing vocabulary. The form and expression is more a derivative of early 20th-century social housing of Europe than a reinterpretation of local housing design. Nonetheless, the project sits comfortably in its milieu and relates better to its site and purpose than the vast majority of similar developments on Nuns' Island. As a new contemporary housing prototype for Montreal, it sets a standard of architectural excellence.

In direct contrast to Hanganu's low-density housing projects on

Nuns' Island, is Mario Biocca's "Cooperative d'habitation l'Escale," built in 1986 on Park Avenue in the Milton Park area. It is a tight, high-density, multi-use, infill project that embodies the essence of meaningful background architecture. The building acknowledges its privileged position on the corner of a city block. It establishes a sympathetic relationship with its immediate neighbours and it grows out of its contextual reality. The building contains two shops at grade level and 15 dwelling units on the upper five floors. To the passerby, the eye is first drawn to a new building; in fact, it is an addition to the smaller adjacent building to the north, and as such, it was conceived as a whole, made up of two distinct parts: one old and one new. Despite some dated Postmodernist appliqués, the façade deals cleverly with the problem of scale manipulation. It is inevitable and somewhat disconcerting to compare this project to its counterpart across the street, an over-blown pseudo-Québecois farmhouse crowned with a plastic orange-coloured roof decorated with make-belief dormers.

If one could describe projects such as Les Habitations Jeanne-Mance, Habitat 67 and the Olympic Village as standing at the heroic end of the housing spectrum in Montreal, then one would place Coopérative Louis-Cyr on St. Jacques Street and Habitations de Grand Pré on de Grand Pré Street at the architecturally and urbanistically silent end. In their self-conscious desire to relegate themselves to a background position, these projects exemplify small "a" architecture at its best. They are certainly non-Modern, insofar as their main urban role is to restructure the block and to be part of a continuum rather than assertion of formal and functional independence from setting. In their desire to contribute to this refiguration process and to integrate themselves totally in the family of neighbouring buildings, they unabashedly resort to the use of the familiar architectural language of the Montreal rowhouse, without any visible attempts to reinterpret it.

Bianchi and Voissard's 1984 housing project on St. André Street, north of Roy Street, follows the same ideological premise. As an infill in a milieu of traditional Montreal triplexes, this project blends in so effortlessly that, except for some subtleties in the details of the façade, one is hardly aware that it is a new addition to the street. Here is the ultimate example of background architecture. In a literal sense, all the traditional elements of domestic architecture of the Plateau Mont Royal are used: the sculpted parapets, the curving external access stairs, the polychrome brickwork and the guillotine windows. It is obvious that the textual re-use of familiar elements implies the loss of critical comment, which the building could have made. Nonetheless, this loss is offset by the project's significant contribution to the "reculturalization" of the street.

Until the 1950s, Montreal had developed and maintained a strong architectural and urban tradition, which was manifest in the institutional buildings, the conventual architecture, the urban villas on the mountain and, importantly, in its medium-density housing. This tradition produced not only a readable and cohesive cityscape, but gave rise to some of the more outstanding residential streets to be found in any North American city. These streets, which Montreal urbanist Jean-Claude Marsan so aptly baptized rues spectacles are joyous places of healthy interaction and unlimited visual interest. In his book, *Montreal in Evolution*, he gives interesting examples of two such streets: Laval Avenue, south of Pine Avenue and de Lorimier Avenue, south of Mount Royal Avenue.

No tradition can be preserved unimpaired and forever within a naturally evolving culture and city. Lifestyles change, socio-economic realities undergo interminable mutations, technology modifies our means of construction. A vital architecture reflects this, avoiding the repetition of the past, comfortable as it may be.

Dan Hanganu has resisted this nostalgic reflex in the design of housing. In his Parc Quesnel project of 1984 on Quesnel Street between Guy and Atwater Streets in Petite Bourgone, no ambiguity about the affirmation of its modernity, there is no giving way to the safety of recycling old forms. The project responds to its context in the broadest and most meaningful sense, for it makes references to the cultural and physical framework within which the work has been conceived. It is an architecture that is concerned with connections, continuity and the interdependency of building and setting, that is to say, the "essence of place."

Here, the traditional elements of the architecture of the housing terraces of the quartier reappear, albeit in an reinterpreted manner. The port-cochere, the polychromy of the façade, the solid massing, the predominance of the vertical over the horizontal and the "punched" windows are elements that are retained and recycled, but not copied. They are the sympathetic quotes from a past architecture.

Imitation, duplication or subservience, all constitute familiar strategies for responding to context and for establishing physical relationships

The Centre d'acceuil Armand-Lavergne on Chapleau Street
on Plateau Mont Royal is a large housing project that blends
in well while serving as a neighbourhood focal point.
Photo by André Blouin.

Houses in les Habitations Notre-Dame repaired some of the
damage caused when east end streets lost their "têtes d'ilot,"
or end buildings, during creation of the Ville Marie Expressway.
Photo by Brian Merrett © copyright.

Houses on St. André Street on the Plateau blend so effortlessly
that one is hardly aware they are in a new addition.
Photo courtesy of Bianchi & Voissard.

Les Cours Ste. Famille is an example of a successful infill
building on a tightly built inner city street.
Courtesy of Mercier, Boyer, Mercier.

within an existing milieu. The analogical reference, in contrast to the above, establishes an association, not based on repetition, but one derived from a process of reinterpretation of existing forms or from the abstraction of a familiar language of architecture. The Centre d'acceuil Armand-Lavergne on Chapleau Street in Plateau Mont Royal by Blouin, Blouin and Associates, completed in 198_, illustrates this latter course of action for urban integration. The centre is both an institution and a large housing development that sits in the middle of an all-residential area. The project reflects its dual nature by being simultaneously a focal point and a background building in its neighbourhood.

If some of the latter-day small housing developments have given Montreal a reason for cautious optimism in architecture, the other significant contributors to the New Architecture, are the less visible but very significant large-scale recycling projects. The conservation/recycling movement began in earnest with the birth of the non-profit housing cooperative movement which led to the saving and conversion of abandoned schools. In general, these first ventures were relatively small, containing 30 dwelling units on the average. They contributed to a new awareness of the urban environment and they demonstrated the economic viability of renovation. Eventually the preservation of larger institutional buildings such as Convent Bon Pasteur and Collège Mont St. Louis, both on Sherbrooke Street east of St. Laurent Boulevard, and the Cours Le Royer in Old Montreal, came about as a matter of course.

Valuable as these projects are, conservation and rehabilitation are passive forms of building that cannot respond to all the changing realities of an urban environment as a new work of architecture can. Not all old buildings can be adapted easily to contemporary needs, incorporate modern facilities or respond to present-day construction and legal constraints. One must look to new buildings and new architecture to make vital, critical and contemporary comments about the city and our common values.

The recent housing projects described here have one thing in common: they have accepted their responsibility to the public spaces of the city, which is to say, they have rediscovered the street, the street that is not merely a road, but a public room of the city and an integral part of urban life.

With the advent of the Modern Movement, the street has been under attack, partly because of the misguided perception that the traditional city was a constraining organism that could no longer fulfill its role, and partly because of the preoccupation with the building as an independent construct, subject only to the authority of its functions. The revisionists of Modernism no longer accept this view.

Suburbia, unfortunately, is still creeping into the odd place in the city, as can be witnessed in a number of the recent redevelopments in Pointe St. Charles, La Coopérative les Tanneries in St. Henri and Les Floralies built on the abandoned railroad yards south of Petite-Bourgogne. These low-density suburban implants constitute a complete reversal in the traditional order of normal city growth.

Good architecture always speaks of its physical and cultural circumstances. It is through architecture that we understand our cities. Good cities are places where the whole adds up to much more than the sum of its parts; where each building is part of the larger whole; where there is a healthy density of use and occupancy to allow for healthy and voluntary interaction; where balance exists between the public and private domains and where its architecture is the embodiment and expression of the common rules of conduct and place.

NOTES ON CONTRIBUTORS

Journalist Dane Lanken is co-author of *Montreal at the Crossroads*.
Norbert Schoenauer is a professor of architecture at McGill University.
Lewis Harris is a city hall reporter at *The Gazette*.
Urban planning specialist Isabel Corral works at the Canadian Centre for Architecture.
Peter Jacobs is a professor of landscape architecture at the Université de Montréal.
Ron Williams is a Montreal landscape architect.
David Brown is an associate professor of urban planning at McGill University.
Architect Derek Drummond is Macdonald professor of architecture at McGill University.
Montreal writer Aline Gubbay is author of *The Mountain and The River*. Her latest book is *A Street Called the Main*.
Ricardo L. Castro is a professor of architecture at McGill University.
Architect Mark London, a former executive director of Heritage Montreal, works for the City of Montreal.
Joshua Wolfe, a former executive director of Heritage Montreal, is a planner with the County of San Diego.
Susan Bronson is a Montreal architect.
Peter Sijpkes is a professor of architecture at McGill University.
Ian MacBurnie is a Montreal architect.
Adrian Sheppard is a professor of architecture at McGill University.

INDEX

2001 University 76, 89
2020 de Maisonneuve 76

Affleck, Ray 41
Alcan 27, 163–65
Alcan architectural lectures 135
Alexis Nihon Plaza 27
Alliance building 123
Amis de la Montagne, Les 59
Appalachian mountains 53
Arnold, Benedict 145
Association de Promotion d'art et d'architecture de Montréal, l' 104
Atwater market 91

Back, Frederic 101–03
Baker, Joe 113
Bank of Montreal 152
Bank of Nova Scotia 89
Banque Nationale de Paris 26, 99, 120, 123, 139
Bastien, Pierre 39
Battlefield Park 62
Baudrillard, Jean 110, 112
Bay, The 26, 74–76
BCE Development Corp. 31
Beaver Lake 57, 62
Belding Corticelli 184, 187
Bennett, Arnold 32, 36–37
Bergeron, Gérmain 104
Berkeley Hotel 113, 162
Bianchi and Voissard 205
Biocca, Mario 205
Bleury-Dorchester 195

Blouin, Blouin, and Associates 209
Bonaventure 76, 195
Bonaventure commuter station 72
Bonaventure expressway 178
Bonaventure Hotel 33
Bonaventure Station 38
Boskey, Sam 36, 39
Bourassa, Napoléon 94
Brother André 98
Brown, Herbert Ames 183
Bumbaru, Dinu 32
Bureau de Transport Métropolitan (BTM) 103

Calder, Alexander 97
Calvino, Italo 196
Camilien Houde parkway 59
Canadian Centre for Architecture (CCA) 8, 36, 116, 118, 142
Canadian Imperial Bank of Commerce 20, 139
Canadian Space agency 33
Cantlie House 24
Caron, Christophe 104
Carter, Joe 177
Cartier, George-Etienne 157
Cartier, Jacques 53, 177
Cartier, Jean 103
Casson, Dollier de 66
Cayouette and Saïa 116, 204
Central Station 71–73
Central Trust building 100
Centre d'acceuil Armand-Lavergne 209

Centre de la Montagne 58
Centre Eaton 31–33, 76, 81, 170
Chambre de Commerce de Montréal 33
Champ de Mars 150
Château Champlain Hotel 21–23, 158
Château Ramezay 145
Chaussegros de Léry 150
Cherrier School 152
Chicago 20, 123, 133, 183
Chinatown 12
Christ Church Cathedral 90, 110, 123
Chrysler building 110
Church of Saint Andrew and Saint Paul, The 150
CIL building 20
Cité du Havre 40
City and District Savings Bank 170
City Arboretum Corp. 31
City council (Montreal) 11, 30–31, 33, 36, 38, 94, 105
Civic Party 33, 38
Clos St-Bernard, Le 115
Cohen, Douglas 35–37
Collège Mont St. Louis 209
Collins, Peter 119
Comité de construction et d'Art sacré de l'Archevêché 156
Commission d'Initiatives et Developpement Culturel (CIDEC) 104
Complexe Desjardins 70, 77, 79–80, 110
Complexe Guy Favreau 77, 79
Concordia University 113, 168, 170
Confederation building 127
Congrégation de Notre Dame 113
Convent Bon Pasteur 209
Cooperative d'habitation l'Escale 205
Coopérative Louis-Cyr 205
Corbusier, Le 133–34, 146
Cormier house 152
Cormier's seaplane hangar 166
Cormier, Ernest 152
Corticelli project 68

Côte St. Paul 177
Cours Le Royer 113, 209
Cours Mont-Royal, Les 26, 81, 165
Cours Sainte-Famille, Les 204
Couvent du Bon Pasteur 113
Cross, Ian 73
Cyr, Louis 97–98

Dallaire, Roger 156
David, Fleury 156
Davis building 27
Dawson College 113
Delorimier baseball grounds 98
Desjardins, Dr. 182
Dickens, Charles 183
Disney, Walt 134
District Advisory Committees (DACs) 33
Dominion Express building 169
Dominion Gallery 99
Dominion Square 98
Dominion Square building 81, 128
Doré, Jean, mayor 29, 33, 35, 66
Drapeau administration 192
Drapeau, Jean, Mayor 11–12, 14–15, 33, 37, 40–41, 46, 48, 200
Dreyfus Group 99
Duplessis, Maurice 200

Eaton's 74–76
Eglise de la Visitation 156–57
Empire State building 110
Etrog 98
Expo 67 12, 20, 40, 61–62, 64–66, 97, 133, 158
Expo Islands 5, 52, 61, 64–65, 69

Faneuil Hall 114–15
Faneuil Market 165
Faubourg, Le 91, 113, 115, 165
Faubourg des Récollets 47, 195
Faubourg Québec 69, 195
Ferme St. Gabriel 178
Ferron, Marcelle 100
Findley and Spence 150

First Quebec Corporation 100
Fish, Michael 36
Flanagan, Barry 100
Floralies, Les 65, 210
Fort de la Montagne 199
Franklin, Benjamin 145
Fuller, Buckminster 97, 133

Gabeline, Donna 8
Gardiner, John 35–38
Gazette, The 7–8
Gehl, Jan 88
Geist, Johann 72
Gnass, Peter 104
Goldberger, Paul 120
Goose Village 40, 184
Goyer, Pierre 36, 39
Graham, Don 65
Grain Elevator No. 1 110, 166
Grain Elevator No. 2 146, 149
Greenspoon, Freedlander and Dunne 200
Griffintown 177, 183–84
Grosvenor Apartment building 150

Habitat 67 64, 133, 205
Habitations de Grand Pré 205
Habitations Jeanne-Mance, Les 199–200, 205
Habitations Notre-Dame, Les 203
Hanganu, Dan 115, 204, 206
Haymarket Square 93
Hebért, Philippe 93–94, 98
Hedman, Richard 169
Hepworth, Barbara 98
Heritage Montreal 7, 32, 48
Hochelaga 53, 177
Hôtel le Palais 168–69
Hough, Michael 65
Huxtable, Ada Louise 28
Hydro-Québec building 110

IBM Canada Ltd. 31, 127
IBM-Marathon building 26, 33, 123, 127–28

Ile Notre Dame 62, 64–65
Ile Ste. Hélène 61–62, 64–65
Indoor City 5, 70–73, 76–82
Industrial Life Tower 26, 99–100, 123–24, 123, 136–39
International Council of Monuments and Sites 149

J.K. Investments 100
Jacobs, Jane 134
Jacobs, Peter 65
Jardin de la Tourbière 65
Jean Talon market 91
Jeanne Mance Park 38
Jensen, Lisa 37
Johnson & Johnson 113, 116
Johnson, J. Seward 99
Johnson, Philip 136
Judith-Jasmin building 169

Karkoukly, Sally 38
Kohn, Pedersen, Fox 120, 127
Kon-Tiki bar 165
Kracauer, J. 100

La Cité 27, 199
La Cité Jardin du Tricentenaire 199
La Coopérative les Tanneries 210
La Ronde 64
Lac des Régates 65–66
Lachine Canal 5, 52, 61, 66–67, 69, 147–49, 175–79, 184, 187
Lafontaine, Louis-Hippolyte 145
Lake Shore Drive Apartments 123
Lake St. Louis 60
Lambert, Phylis 36
Lamothe, Monsieur 57
Landau, Robert 35–37
Lanken, Dane 8
Las Vegas 176
Lash, Christopher 152
Laurentian Hotel 158
Laurentian lakes 66
Laurentian mountains 53, 60
Legault, Guy 203

Lever House 152
Little Burgundy 41
Little Italy 84, 87
Little St. Pierre River 177
Loge Peuple 184
London, Mark 7, 65
London [England] 11, 68, 72, 104

Mackay Pier 64
Maison Alcan 27, 100, 113, 116, 124, 136, 162, 165, 175
Maison des Coopérants 26, 110, 123, 128, 139
Maison George-Etienne Cartier 156–57
Maisonneuve Park 99, 199
Marathon Realty Co. Ltd. 31
Marchand, Denis 31–32
Marchand, J. Omer 113, 156
Marquess of Dufferin 93
Marsan, Jean-Claude 12, 66, 108, 206
Mason, Raymond 99
Master plan 11, 15, 18, 30, 32–33, 40, 42, 45–49, 58, 65, 67, 191, 196
McDonald's [restaurant] 152
McDonald, Nick 48
McGill University 12, 54, 72, 149
McGill, Peter 103
Melançon, Pierre-Yves 39
Mercier, Boyer and Mercier 203
Mercure, Desnoyers 113
Métropolis 165
Mies van der Rohe 123, 127, 133, 158, 161
Ministry of Cultural Affairs [Quebec] 150, 170
Monkland Theatre 14
Montgomery, Richard 145
Montreal Botanical Garden 57, 62, 99
Montreal Citizens' Movement (MCM) 14–15, 29–33, 35–39, 42, 46, 48–49, 192–93
Montreal Museum of Fine Arts 89, 113, 168, 173

Montreal Royals 98
Montreal Urban Community 103
Montreal Urban Community Transit Corp. 73
Moore, Henry 98
Mother House of the Grey Nuns 149
Mount Royal 19, 30, 33, 52–54, 57–60, 62
Mount Royal Cemetery 54
Mount Royal Hotel 113, 158
Mount Royal summit lookout 60
Mount Royal, Town of 62

Nelson's column 93
Nervi, Pier Luigi 127
New Sherbrooke apartment building 113, 173–75
New York City 20, 24, 62, 104, 110, 136, 152
Niederman, Zoya 100
Northern Electric 184
Notman, William 179
Notre Dame Cathedral 133
Notre-Dame-des-Neiges Cemetery 54
Nuns' Island 204–05

Ogilvy Mills 184
Old Montreal 46, 69, 112–13, 183, 195, 209
Olmsted, Frederick Law 54, 57
Olympic Stadium 97–98, 109, 116
Olympic Village 199–200, 205
Opération 10,000 logements 41, 203
Opération 20,000 logements 41, 193, 203
Opération 300 logements 203
Otto, Frei 133
Ouellet, Reeves and Allain 201–03
Outremont 59, 104, 115
Overdale 14, 35–38, 146
Overdale Tenants' Association 37

Pape, Gordon 8

Papineau, Louis-Joseph 103
Parc Agro-alimentaire 65
Parc Dante 87
Parc Ladauversière 87
Parc Quesnel 206
Paris [France] 11–12, 133, 176
Parks Canada 67, 157
Pastier, John 8
Paul de Chomedey Sieur de Maisonneuve 93
Pei, I.M. 127, 158
Pelletier, Robert 98
Petite-Bourgogne 200–03, 206, 210
Piste Gilles Villeneuve 65
Place Bonaventure 21–23, 31, 76, 78, 158
Place Canada Trust 119–20, 124
Place d'Armes 76, 93
Place d'Youville 145
Place de la Cathédrale 26, 80
Place des Arts 46, 76, 101–03, 195
Place du Canada 21–23, 31
Place Frontenac 199
Place Guy Favreau 80
Place Jacques Cartier 146, 149
Place Mercantile 26–27, 168, 173
Place Montréal Trust 15, 26, 76, 80, 115, 139, 158
Place Victoria 20
Place Ville Marie 11, 20, 23, 30, 52, 71–72, 78, 80–81, 110, 133, 139, 146, 158, 161
Plains of Abraham 62
Plateau Mont Royal 141, 205, 209
Pointe à Callières 178
Pointe St. Charles 6, 176, 178–79, 182–88, 210
Pont de la Concorde 64
Prodevco Immobilière 31, 33
Provincial Bank of Canada 169

Quebec City 62
Queen Elizabeth Hotel 158
Queen Victoria 93
Queen's Hotel 38

Queen's Hotel, The 14, 38, 144, 158, 166, 170

Radburn plan 199
Radio-Canada building 12
Ramezay, Claude de 145
Redpath Sugar 184, 187
Referendum 11
Regent Theatre 14
Riesman, Eugene 100
Riopelle, Jean-Paul 97
Ritz-Carlton Hotel 38, 158
Robinson, Jackie 98
Rockhill Apartments 199
Rodin, Olidon 98
Rother, Bland and Trudeau 200
Rotrand, Marvin 36, 39
Royal George apartments 113, 170

Safdie, Moishe 133
Saint-Jean, Casimir 149
San Francisco 169
Save Montreal heritage group 31
School of Architecture, Université de Montréal 64
Schwartz's 46
Service d'habitation de Montréal, Le 195, 200, 203
Sevigny, Marcel 36
Shaughnessy House 117–18
Simpson's 76
Sir Robert Peel [condominium block] 14, 166–67
Skidmore, Owens, and Merrill 127
Slovenia 46
Smith House 60
Sollogoub, Nicolas 101–03
South Shore 177, 179
St. Henri 183, 187, 193, 210
St. Hubert 33
St. Jacques Cathedral 169
St. Jean Baptiste Church 149
St. Joseph de Montréal 156
St. Joseph's Oratory 52, 98
St. Lambert 179–82

St. Laurent 195
St. Lawrence River 53–54, 57–58, 149, 177–79, 182, 204
St. Lawrence Seaway 67, 184
St. Léonard 84, 87
St. Louis Square 146
St. Pierre River 177–78
Ste. Cunégonde 156
Stein, Clarence 199
Stelco Steel 184, 187
Stern, Max 98
Stern, Robert 135
Sun Life building 20, 81
Sunshine Garment Company 46

Teleglobe Canada 31
Terre des Hommes 65
Terry, Quinlan 141
Théâtre Empire 165
Todd, Frederick 62
Trans-Canada Highway 130
Trois Rivières 77

"Underdale" 37
Université de Montréal 31–32, 54, 64–65, 152
Université du Québec à Montréal (UQAM) 46, 168–69

Van Horne mansion 12, 41, 144
Venturi, Robert 134, 176
Verdun 177
Victoria Bridge 179
Victoriatown 40
Victoriaville 184
Victorin, Marie 57
Vieux Port 61, 65, 67–69
Vieux Port Committee 69
Viger, Jacques 101–03
Ville Emard 177
Ville Marie expressway 12, 41, 203
Vitruvius 115–16
Vivot, Lea 99

Warhol, Andy 110

Webb & Knapp 23
Wertheimer, Esther 100
West Edmonton Mall 77–78
Westmount 41, 59, 177
Westmount Square 27, 123–24, 133, 146, 158, 161
Whyte, William 79, 88
Williams, Ron 99
Windsor, Le 165
Windsor Hotel 38, 158, 165
World Trade Centre [Montreal] 112, 168, 173
World Trade Center [New York] 110, 136

York Cinema 31
York-Hannover project 31
Young, John 98

Zeckendorf, William 23

DOSSIER QUÉBEC SERIES

LIFE OF THE PARTY
Gérard Fortin and Boyce Richardson

**THE MILTON PARK AFFAIR:
CANADA'S LARGEST CITIZEN-DEVELOPER
CONFRONTATION**
Claire Helman

**A MAN OF SENTIMENT:
THE MEMOIRS OF PHILIPPE-JOSEPH AUBERT DE GASPÉ
1786–1871**
Translated, annotated, and introduced by Jane Brierley

**SWINGING IN PARADISE:
THE STORY OF JAZZ IN MONTREAL**
John Gilmore

**WHO'S WHO OF JAZZ IN MONTREAL:
RAGTIME TO 1970**
John Gilmore

**GRASSROOTS, GREYSTONES, AND GLASS TOWERS:
MONTREAL URBAN ISSUES AND ARCHITECTURE**
Brian Demchinsky, editor